Door to Door Re

The Complete Guide to
Door Knocking for Listings

Door to Door Real Estate Prospecting:
The Complete Guide to Door Knocking for Listings

By Linda Schneider

Agents on Fire Publications
San Diego, CA

Door to Door Real Estate Prospecting: The Complete Guide to Door Knocking for Listings
Agents on Fire Publications
Copyright ©2014 by Linda Schneider, author
All rights reserved. First edition 2014
ISBN 978-1497400191

Agents on Fire Publications
7074 Belle Glade Lane
San Diego, CA 92119
contact@agentsonfire.com

Contents

Preface

Chapter 1: Realities of Door Knocking/FAQs   1

Answers FAQs about door knocking as a prospecting approach. Puts you in the shoes of a successful door knocker.

Chapter 2: Door Knocking Strategies   31

Learn variations on door knocking, including continuous knocking, farm knocking, and special purpose door knocking strategies.

Chapter 3: Harvesting Leads   55

Focus on questions about leads—who they are, how to dig them out, who to spend time on, and who to drop.

Chapter 4: The Inner Game of Door Knocking   65

Address your mindset for prospecting, with specific exercises for bolstering confidence for door knocking.

Chapter 5: Door Knocking Scripts   79

Get a variety of opening phrases, questions, conversations, and sales language needed to uncover leads and get listings.

Chapter 6: Fanatical Follow Up   95

Focus on filling the pipeline and converting leads

Summary: Set Up Your Door Knocking Plan   105

Walk through a process for developing a door knocking plan.

Bonus Chapter: Openhanded Selling   109

How to sell without sounding or feeling like a salesperson.

Preface

No other real estate prospecting approach creates as much controversy as door knocking. Some agents have an almost venomous dislike of it. They would rather have a root canal than knock on a stranger's door to ask for business. They are often quick to belittle agents who choose door knocking as their core prospecting approach.

On the other hand, there are agents who enjoy door knocking and go quietly about the business of raking in listings to the tune of hundreds of thousands of dollars in personal income over the life of their business. We seldom hear from them, because they're busy quietly making money. A few top agents in your own company are probably successful door knockers, even if you don't know it.

In between these two extremes are many agents who, like you, are on the fence about door knocking or considering door knocking for the first time. You want door knocking to work so you can generate listings. But you're not sure about it. Does it really work? What should you say? What do the experts do? You have a lot of questions, you want assurances, and you want it to be easy.

Well, door knocking is easy and it does work, as you'll discover from the stories and interviews in this book. As for assurances, door knocking has as much likelihood of success as any other prospecting approach—the more you do it, the better it works. Take Froy Candelario, for instance, an agent out of the Los Angeles area. He would knock four to six hours per day, resulting in a personal income close to a half million dollars annually. (See interview inside.)

* * *

My story with door knocking began when I was a brand new real estate agent in Salt Lake City, Utah in 1984. I had hung my license with one of those old school brokers who could pull business out of thin air through hard work. She taught me just one strategy—go knock on doors. She handed me Tom Hopkins' book, *How to Master the Art of Listing and Selling Real Estate,* and enrolled me in a seminar to hear a relatively new real estate speaker at the time, named Mike Ferry.

Between Hopkins, Ferry, and my broker, I assumed a no-nonsense "go where the sellers are" mind-set to building a real estate business. Armed with determination and plenty of time as a new agent, I started a program of door knocking.

Fourteen days into my program, I listed my first home—a tidy Tudor in an upscale Salt Lake City neighborhood called The Avenues. The scene unfolded like this: I knocked. The owner answered. He listened politely to my spiel, and said *"Yes, we are planning to sell. Would you like to come in and see the home?"* I was stunned. At first I thought he might be joking, and I suavely blurted, *"Are you serious?"* Fortunately he had a sense of humor and we hit it off. Later when I asked why he would hire an obviously new agent to sell his home, he said *"I believe in rewarding hard work."*

When I shared this success at our next office meeting, one of the more experienced agents (let's call him Mr. Sunshine) put his arms behind his head, leaned back in his chair, and graced me with the opinion that I was lucky, because door knocking is usually a waste of time. Moreover, he said that it gave people the message that I was desperate, contributed to the negative reputation of real estate agents, and was akin to being a used car salesman. His advice was to start networking instead.

BLAM! I was shattered. Here was a top agent putting me down, making me feel small and stupid. I was embarrassed and too surprised to know what to say. I went back to my cubicle, feeling demoralized.

Thankfully, my terrific broker came to the rescue. She brought me to her office and gave me a verbal slap upside the head. Her advice has stuck with me ever since:

Whatever prospecting you do, she said, is all about your energy. People see your enthusiasm and they believe in you. It's like walking down the street smiling for no particular reason. People smile back at you. They feel your energy. Door knocking doesn't work for people like (Mr. Sunshine) because he doesn't believe in it. You do. You've seen it work. I bet that if you start door knocking again, you'll get another listing before (Mr. Sunshine) does.

With that shrewd challenge I hit the doors again, determined to beat Mr. Sunshine to the punch. It took me another three weeks, but I did land my next listing before Mr. Sunshine. It was a vacant home that I had run across in my first week of door knocking. Often door knocking is like that...the listing you get is from your door knocking efforts weeks or months or sometimes years before.

***

My goal in writing this book is not to change hard opinions about door knocking, but to give those who want to door knock the tools to get off the fence and do it well.

In this book, you'll find stories from people who make over a half-million dollars annually from door knocking, as well as stories from average agents who are just getting started. You'll find answers to all of your questions about door knocking, like: "How long does it take to get a listing?" "What do I say?" "Where should I knock?" and "How do I convert door leads?" You'll read about different door knocking strategies, get scripts for finding and converting leads, and find ideas for motivating yourself. Most importantly, you'll have a prospecting approach you can take to the bank.

Good luck and happy hunting!

Linda Schneider

Chapter 1: The Realities of Door Knocking – FAQs

What does it feel and look like to door knock? What should you do and say? What's real and not real? Chapter One addresses the myths and realities of door knocking:

- Why Door Knock?
- The Devil Is in the Details
- First Day Door Knocking
- Will I Have to Become a Salesperson?
- Develop a Listing Agent Mindset
- Best Personality for Door Knocking
- What to Wear
- What to Hand Out
- Danger and Door Knocking
- How Many Doors to Reach My Listing Goals?
- How Long Does It Take to Knock on 100 Doors?
- What Is the Best Time of Day to Door Knock?
- How Much Money Can I Make—Is It Worth It?
- When Will I Get My First Listing?
- Is Door Knocking Legal?
- How Do Home Owners React?

Why Door Knock?

Imagine there is a treasure buried somewhere in your neighborhood. There's no X marking the spot, no map, and no clues. The only way to find this treasure is to persistently knock on every door in the neighborhood and ask the owner if the treasure is there. The only thing you know for sure is that if you knock on enough doors, you are absolutely guaranteed to find the treasure. Would you do it? Would you knock on those doors and ask?

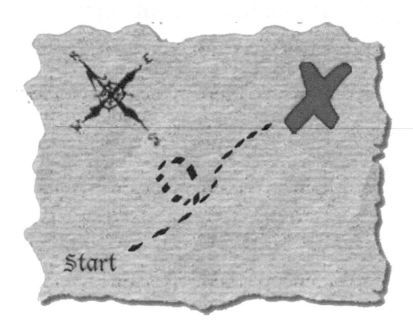

Ultimately, that is the question that matters in door knocking. It's not what you say, how you look, or what your experience is. It's "Will you do it?" Because if you will, you will uncover treasure in the form of *listings* worth hundreds of thousands—possibly millions—in personal income over the lifetime of your business.

All you need is persistence, belief, and enthusiasm. Add a little knowledge and skill and you'll do it faster.

Before we dive into door knocking, I want you to examine your interest in door knocking. Why, with all the other prospecting approaches out there, would you want to do door knocking?

After all, it's strictly old-school, face-to-face selling. There is no high-tech short cut.

Instead of door knocking, you could do direct mail, which takes less effort and involves no rejection. You could focus entirely on networking, which has proven to generate business all across the real estate world. You could do telemarketing to reach more people

2

faster without ever leaving your office. You could advertise in targeted publications and seduce people into calling you. Why would you door knock?

Other than the money, I can think of eight compelling reasons to door knock. Door knocking...

1. Is completely free.
2. Consistently generates listings.
3. Provides excellent physical exercise.
4. Creates a distinct presence in your geographic farm.
5. Has a mild rejection level compared to telemarketing.
6. Does not require a large list or a sphere of influence to be successful.
7. Does not require listings to get more listings.
8. Requires no preparation—you can get up and start prospecting now.

Of course, there are disadvantages, too.

-   You have to physically work; you can't assign door knocking to an assistant or put it in the mail and pay for it to attract sellers.
-   You can't hint and hope—you have to learn solid consultative selling skills.
-   With door knocking, you are forced to look rejection in the eye, rather than hanging up on it or hoping they call you.

I believe the pros outweigh the cons, especially when preparation and training virtually eliminate the disadvantages.

Keep in mind that doing door knocking doesn't negate any other form of prospecting. You can still do direct response mail, networking, internet leads, and so on. You probably should do more than one form of prospecting, and can easily incorporate little guerilla marketing tactics into your business on a daily basis. If you want some ideas for continuous marketing, go to Amazon.com and grab a copy of my ebooklet: *The Constant Agent: 32 Proven Real Estate Marketing ideas to Build into Your Business Daily.*

The Devil Is in the Details

What does door knocking look like in practice? At one level, you know the answer: You knock on a door, ask a few questions, get an answer, and move on to the next door.

But the devil is in the details. Some of the daunting details behind successful door knocking include what to say, how to dress, how to ask for appointments, how to track results, how to motivate yourself, how to improve results, what to hand out, how to handle rejection, how to follow up, and most importantly, how to convert leads to appointments.

Door knocking is not rocket science. About 70% of it is simple persistence, and 30% is technique, more or less. That's not to say you should ignore the technique and simply plow forward. Mastering technique can remove your fear, improve your odds, and shorten your learning curve.

The interesting thing about door-to-door is that once you begin, you find yourself in spontaneous situations for which there is no script.

For instance, instead of saying *yes* to your opening question, they might answer, *"Maybe, why do you ask?"* Instead of saying *no*, they might say *"Well, we're not exactly moving."* What does that mean...yes or no?

And there are physical challenges, too. How will you react when seven yapping Chihuahuas rush the door and the owner won't quiet them? What will you do when someone starts yelling at you? How do you handle yourself when the homeowner wants to invite you in?

The best preparation is to know your opening scripts like the back of your hand and practice follow-on questions to common "off script" scenarios, like those just mentioned. For detailed help with your door sales skills, refer to **Chapter 5: Door Knocking Scripts**, and **Bonus Chapter: Openhanded Selling**. Beyond that, the best training is to get out there and get your feet wet, make mistakes, and have fun. Here is an example of how easy it can be to get started:

***

First Day
by Sarah Maloney, Johnson Realty, Michigan

I love door knocking now, but before I started, I was pretty sure I'd hate it. I only started doing it because of an office listing challenge.

I chose a neighborhood close, but not too close to my home. I didn't want to talk to people I knew, just in case I made a fool of myself.

The first day I drove around the neighborhood looking for just the right house to begin with. Really I was just dragging my feet. Finally, I parked under a shady tree and went up to a door. I had terrible butterflies in my stomach like I was going on a date.

As soon as I knocked, I realized I had forgotten my business cards. Oh, well. Too late now. I waited a respectable minute and no one came to the door. Should I knock again? I decided to go on to the next door.

This time an elderly lady answered. I forgot to smile, but went through my script. She invited me in to look around, but wasn't planning on moving. She just liked the company. But she did tell me about a neighbor who passed away and I should talk to the kids. No she didn't have the phone number for the kids, but their last name was Kelmann and she thought they lived in the area.

Next door, no. Next door, no. Then a large man with no neck and tattoos up and down his arms. I thought briefly that I should turn around and walk away now. But I plastered a sunny smile on my face and went through my script. He said, "Oh, thanks for coming by, but we just moved in a few months ago." Nice as could be.

Next door, no. Next door, no. And so it went. Anyway, in all that first day, I knocked for an hour and met seven people before quitting. I only got the one lead to follow up on, but I survived and no one was mean to me. In fact, just the opposite. People were really nice.

***

Will I Have to Become a Salesperson?

The field of real estate sales attracts many people who don't like selling. They like serving, mostly in the form of advising, counseling, transacting, and guiding. But none of these will result in a high-income real estate business without the drive to ask for business as often as possible. More specifically, you need the drive to *find someone to ask*, and the *ability to ask*. One is prospecting. The other is selling.

If you try to serve your way to getting clients, you'll be exhausted and frustrated. You'll give away tons of CMA's, drive buyers around for days and days, and spend countless hours in front of the computer doing unpaid research—all in the hope that they'll "get" how good you are at service and then hire you. Selling *and* serving is far more profitable than serving alone.

But how do you convince someone to hire you for your service when you haven't demonstrated it yet? Great question. The answer is that you learn how to sell correctly, by being a sales consultant.

What is a sales consultant?

You don't have to be a pushy jerk to be a great salesperson. Great salespeople are heroes. Have you ever shopped for a car, TV, boat, computer, or phone, and you were so glad you found a knowledgeable salesperson to help you? And that knowledgeable salesperson asked you all the right questions to help you clarify your needs and come to the right decision? And maybe they helped you over the edge by saying, *"Well, shall we wrap it up for you?"* And afterwards you were so happy and grateful.

Selling means asking questions that help people clarify their concerns and make decisions...for themselves, not because you twisted their arms. It means bringing value through the very process of selling—by asking questions they don't know to ask, helping them evaluate the answers, and then giving them an opportunity to say *yes* to your closing questions.

You're the real estate hero they're looking for.

So, yes, you will have to become a salesperson to the extent that you will have to learn how to ask questions that help people make decisions that are right for them.

Bonus Chapter: Openhanded Selling
I highly encourage you to read the Bonus Chapter at the end of this book. There you will find a methodology that has been designed to help you become a fantastic salesperson, without selling your soul or becoming something you're not.

Develop a Listing Agent Mindset

The primary purpose of door knocking is to generate listings, so if you've been working mostly with buyers up to this point, you may need to shift your mindset. Having a listing agent mindset will put you in the right frame to attract and capture listings when you have the opportunity.

How to Be a Listing Agent

The decision to become a listing agent begins with a shift of focus. There is inherently more sales challenge involved in convincing a home owner to part with 5% or 6% of their hard-earned equity than in convincing a buyer to go look at houses for free. For that reason, you must believe you are worth the money you will be asking the seller to pay. You must be committed to being a valuable asset to sellers. You must learn to have crucial sales conversations around money and other seller concerns.

Being a listing agent also requires a commitment of your energy. The time and money you were spending on finding and working with buyers will now be invested in finding and winning listings. Your attention will be put into learning the contracts used in listing property, mastering your listing presentation, recognizing the problems you'll need to be ready to solve, understanding the legalities involved in transferring real estate, developing your service provider team, and creating procedures for running a listing business.

You will also become knowledgeable about your market, such as senior communities, neighborhoods, expireds, fsbo's, coastal homes, etc. You will have a USP (unique selling proposition) that positions you in your market as the obvious expert.

List to Last

As a listing agent, you have greater control. Consider that sellers (unlike buyers) never have their loan turned down, seldom get seduced away from you by another agent, generally don't change their minds once they've listed, don't become unqualified because they decided to buy a new car at the last moment, and almost never get priced out of the market due to interest rate changes. When you have the listing, buyers may come and go, but you still have the listing.

Every listing you take can generate one to three additional transactions, putting a higher value on your efforts to land one listing than your efforts to put one buyer into a home. Listings are like neon signs advertising you. Potential sellers notice you. Buyers call you directly. You double-side some of your own listings and work with a few well-qualified buyers, while generating even more listings. Your listings work for you while you work on generating more listings. Buyer's agents do not have that luxury.

By becoming a listing agent, you will earn more money than most doctors, lawyers, pilots, and professors. You will make more money than most buyer agents. You will have more freedom to come and go than almost any other professional, and you will have a saleable product that will continue to support you after you exit your business.

When you start door knocking, be mentally and physically prepared to get a listing *on the spot*—it will happen. Even if you don't have all of your systems worked out, even if you don't feel "ready," stay focused on being a listing agent. Be thinking about your USP and how valuable you can be to this home owner. When you're mentally prepared, you attract home owners who sense your conviction. Listings will happen.

What Is the Best Personality for Door Knocking?

The perfect personality for door knocking is someone who is shy, uncertain of themselves, and soft-spoken...or outgoing, verbose, confident, and brassy. In other words, there is no perfect personality. Sure, the gregarious and beautiful people have an edge. They always do. Thank goodness most of the world functions without all of us being gregarious and beautiful. There's plenty of room for everyone.

Being outgoing, charming, and charismatic do not make door knocking work. Professionalism makes it work. Smiling, looking relaxed, and sticking to a script make it work. Forget the "perfect personality." There's only an "effective approach," and the good news is that through practice and experience, everyone can develop their own effective approach.

The best way to be when you door knock is *enthusiastic*, with a sunny smile and a dead-certain attitude. The more certain you sound about what you're saying, the more people will be attracted to your energy. And even if you are not (yet) certain, just fake it. Have a big smile, speak boldly, and use well-rehearsed scripts. They'll never know you're unsure of yourself as long as you are enthusiastic.

What Should I Wear?

As a practical matter, when door knocking…

Dress professionally, but not in a suit. Call it business casual or classy tourist. Women should choose dressy slacks or Capri pants with an attractive, comfortable shirt or jacket appropriate for the weather. If you are comfortable and professional looking in a casual summer dress, wear that.

In the heat of the summer, I typically wear light slacks and a sleeveless blouse. In winter I layer, so I can strip down when I get too hot. A friend of mine wears "fancy sweat suits"—the kind that rich ladies wear to walk their teacup poodles (in the movies). Avoid sexy: no cleavage, short skirts, or skin-tight pants.

Men should wear casual slacks and a Polo or light dress shirt, tucked in (if the waistline allows it). In winter a sports jacket or blazer over a sweater works well, or a nice ski parka in the coldest areas. Wear a tie or not, but a full suit is overkill in most markets.

No - Overdressed

Yes - Casual

11

Wear super comfortable shoes. Black tennis shoes or comfortable loafers work well. In summer, I wear a favorite pair of sandals that are made for walking and look somewhat dressy. In winter, I have a pair of Rockports for women that are like warm butter on my feet. You may not win fashion awards with your door-knocking shoes, but you will make a ton of money by being able to knock longer.

Little extras. I wear earthy **jewelry**, like brass earrings and a hand-crafted necklace. It makes me look less "salesy." But you can do just as well with no jewelry or with fancy jewelry. I also sometimes carry a **clipboard**, but it's also not necessary. The clipboard holds flyers, cards, and a notepad, and gives me a place to attach my pen, glasses, and car key. But I've been just as effective simply carrying business cards, sticking a pen behind my ear, and putting my key in my pocket. Ladies, don't take a **purse**—it makes you look like a church lady or a social worker. Nothing wrong with that, but it's not the image you're trying to convey as a busy, go-getter real estate agent.

Phones are optional. I like leaving mine behind so I'm not distracted.

Always wear a name tag. Your company name will go under the radar, but the fact that you have a name tag will register and add to your credibility. I also wear a **lanyard** around my neck with my lockbox key card attached. It makes me look more "official," but it's not necessary—don't waste time looking for a lanyard if you don't have one already.

What Should I Hand Out?

When I first started door knocking, I never handed out a flyer. I still prefer not using flyers since I tend to drop them as I'm fumbling to hand one over. However, there are times when a flyer is useful, including the following:

- To keep track of how many doors you've knocked on. If you print 100 flyers and hand one out at each door, then when you're out of flyers, you know you've done 100 doors. It doesn't matter what's on the flyers. They're for you to keep track of your numbers, not for the home owner to read.

- To do a "soft meet" of the neighbors when you intend to farm the area. I like to produce an open house invitation flyer and walk it around to a few hundred doors in the days leading up to an open house. This is especially effective with new listings, because people are curious. When using an invitation flyer, you will likely get distracted by talking about the content of the flyer, so don't forget to steer the conversation back to asking about their moving plans.

Sample hand-out item.

- To do the same job as direct response mail. I find that using direct response mail in conjunction with door knocking is very effective in a farm. However, not everyone can afford to mail hundreds of pieces every month. In that case, flyer drops on door steps may be just as effective for a fraction of the cost. Use direct response flyers *in addition to* door knocking, not *instead of* it. Dropping flyers without door knocking is just a waste of time.

- You may want to have someone else deliver flyers for you while you keep knocking. See **Chapter 2: Door Knocking Strategies** for a complete farming plan that uses direct response mail and flyers to augment your door knocking campaign.

Keep in mind that flyers can be more distracting than useful. By handing over a flyer, you create a conversation piece. Now instead of asking about their plans and moving on to the next door, you are wasting precious minutes chatting about the contents of the flyer.

Danger and Door Knocking

Anytime you go to someone's front door, you run the risk of meeting something unsavory behind the door. Most of the time you find friendly folks, occasionally irritated folks, and very rarely weird or scary folks.

If you're a woman and you get the sense that the situation is unsafe or odd, leave immediately. Never accept an invitation to go into someone's house unless you are *confident* that they're harmless. Usually those invitations only happen after standing at the door and having an in-depth conversation first, giving you a chance to get a feel for the situation.

Women, if you're invited in by a man alone, use common sense. If you're not sure of the situation, you can always stand at the door and look around from that position. If there are dogs that don't seem under control, or seem threatening, you might not want to go in. If there are several men inside (for whatever reason), you might not want to go in. If a man or woman gives you a weird "vibe," you might not want to go in. These situations don't happen very often, but be aware. You knock on enough doors, and you'll encounter them occasionally.

Men, you have the opposite problem. You must often take pains to look less threatening to women who answer the door. You must stand well-back from the door at all times, and you will seldom be asked inside by the woman of the house unless her husband is at home, or as one agent says, "You look particularly harmless."— whatever that means!

Knocking with a partner is a great solution for both men and women. Men should knock with a woman partner, because when two men show up at the door it doubles the intimidation factor for the home owner. Women can knock with either a man or woman partner.

When partner knocking, you can either go together to each door or each of you take a side of the street, if the neighborhood is laid out to allow for that. But partner knocking is much less common than individual knocking, so don't let a lack of a partner stop you from knocking.

Dogs

If you are very afraid of dogs, you may want to reconsider door knocking, because you will encounter dogs.

Even if you are not afraid of dogs, keep in mind that dogs are loud and occasionally aggressive. Sometimes a dog will jump at the storm door, barking furiously. If the owner does not immediately grab the dog and quiet it, simply turn around and walk away. You don't owe them an explanation and you don't have to be polite if they're not. You can't compete with the noise and agitation of a barking dog.

On occasion, I believe some owners allow their dogs to bark aggressively out of a misguided sense of personal space, akin to road rage by drivers who make aggressive moves to threaten other drivers who've encroached on their "personal space."

The size of the dog doesn't matter, either. The only dog that ever bit me was a tiny terrier whose owner thought it was being cute. Like many home owners, he had let his dog out, saying *"Oh, he's friendly."* These owners don't mean any harm, but may not realize that some dogs think you're the mailman.

I love dogs, but I prefer not to meet them at the door. If I hear a dog barking on the other side of the door, and the owner is not saying anything to the dog before opening the door, I'm already walking away. I just don't deal with it any more.

How Many Doors to Reach My Goals?

A nice rule of thumb is that the number of listings you get for the year from door knocking equals *roughly* twice the number of people you speak to each day. (Numbers per day are based on a 5-day work week for 46 weeks.) So getting 20 deals would mean talking to roughly 40 people each day. Here are the numbers:

- **10 listings/yr = 15 to 20 contacts/day**
- **20 listings/yr = 35 to 40 contacts/day**

The truth is that over time you'll need to speak with fewer people to maintain your listing numbers. Think of door knocking in your first years as front-loading your business so you can knock less (or not at all if you follow up well) in later years.

How many doors is that?

Agents across North America, and even some in Australia, report that that only 20 to 35 percent of people are home during the day, depending on which time and day of the week they knock.

Suppose your goal is 10 listings per year, and you need to speak with 20 people per day. How many doors is that? If you knock evenings and Saturday mornings, you might be able to reach 20 people in 60 doors (33% at home). But if you knock mid-day during the work week, you might reach 20 people in 100 doors (20% at home).

Why does this matter? Because time is money and having to knock on another 40 doors might mean another hour of knocking.

Calculate your door knocking goals

Fill in the blanks below to calculate the number of doors you'll need to knock on to reach your listing goals in your first year of knocking:

1. How many listings do you want to get from door knocking over the next 12 months?

    _____ (goal)

2. Multiply your goal by two:

    _____ (goal) x 2 = _____ (contacts/day)

3. Divide number of contacts needed by response rate:

    _____ (contacts/day) ÷ .20 (response rate) = _____ (doors/day)

Example:

1. **10** (goal)
2. **10** (goal) x 2 = **20** (contacts/day)
3. **20** (contacts/day) ÷ .20 (response rate) = **100** (doors/day)

You can play around with the response rate, raising it to .30 and so on. Clearly the higher the response rate, the fewer doors you'll need to knock, which translates to less time. You won't know your actual response rate until you've been out door knocking for a week and can take an average over all days of the week and times of the day.

Ultimately the question everyone wants to know at this point is how long does it take to knock on 100 doors?

How Long Does It Take to Knock on 100 Doors?

The quick answer is 2 to 3 hours.

Personally, I knock at a rate of 40 doors per hour. It takes me 2.5 hours to knock on 100 doors, and I get a response rate of about 33%, which means I speak to around 33 people every 100 doors, or 33 people in 2.5 hours.

Some agents can knock 100 doors in less than two hours. Others struggle to get to 100 doors in an entire day. Darla Jenson in an Atlanta suburb says, *"Our lots are so big I can only knock 15 doors an hour!"*

You can increase your door knocking averages by selecting higher density neighborhoods, walking faster, talking faster, and avoiding hilly areas.

Can you get to 200 or even 300 doors in a day? Sure, if you have the time and stamina. I'm pooped after 2.5 hours and 100 doors. On the other hand, some massively high-volume agents can go for 4 to 5 hours/day, knocking on up to 400 doors.

Just in case you're thinking "No one could do that," consider that a mail carrier with a foot route walks 4 to 5 hours per day, covers around 10 miles/16 kilometers, and delivers mail to about 150 homes/hour, or a total of 600 to 750 homes. You can walk half as much and make 5 times the income!

How long will it take to knock on the number of doors needed to reach *your* goals? You won't know for sure until you try it out for a week or so and track these figures:

- # of door knocked
- # of hours spent knocking
- # of people answering
- # of leads generated

What Is the Best Time of Day to Door Knock?

Anytime. I used to try targeting my times to increase my response rate, but found that different people are home at different times. Evenings and weekends are excellent for reaching day workers, but many stay-at home moms and dads are happier to talk in the day than they are in the evening. Working people often come home for lunch and don't mind answering a quick question about real estate, while weekends are great for catching couples when they're relaxed.

Don't bother with trying to target times at first. Just get started. You can play with times and days of the week later when you know your numbers better.

How Much Money Can I Make—and Is It Worth It?

Door knocking allows you—a competent agent—to generate 10 to 20 listings per year from scratch, using no money, having no relationships in the community, and even being brand new in business. In addition, you'll have spin-off business from buyers and sellers at the rate of one or two additional deals for each listing. That means if you generate 10 listings from door knocking, it's very likely you'll do 20 or more transactions (sides) for the year.

Over time, you'll have gathered so many future leads and new relationships into your database that eventually you'll double or triple your business without increasing your door knocking. Is that worth it to you? Let's look at an example.

Income from Door Knocking (Based on $200,000 Average Price Point)

Below I've listed some rough calculations of profit based on a $200,000 average home price at a 2.5% gross commission, before splits. *This is for example purposes only.* YOUR actual numbers will be higher or lower, depending on your average commission check.

Clearly you could easily double these figures in some high-priced marketplaces.

Note: Sphere of Influence (SOI) calls are included in this example to remind you that door knocking by itself does not generate listings. Follow-up generates listings. Door knocking generates leads.

Example

Knocking 5 days/week, 46 weeks, $200,000 average price, 2.5% gross commission ($5,000), 33% response rate:

- 30 contacts/day (90 doors, 2 hours) + 3 lead follow-up calls/day = $60,000 per year gross. [1 listing per month*] Total: 3 hours of prospecting and follow-up per day.

- 40 contacts/day (120 doors, 3 hours) + 10 lead follow up calls = $150,000 per year gross. [2.5 listings per month] Total: 4.5 hours of prospecting/follow-up.

- 60 contacts/day (180 doors, 4 hours) + 15 lead follow up calls = $270,000 per year gross. [4.5 listings per month] Total: 6 hours of prospecting/follow-up.

21

* The number of actual listings you get from any particular number of contacts depends on the strength of your listing presentation, your ability to convert leads to appointments, your follow-up strategy, and your marketplace. This example uses averages as reported by agents.

Notice the jump in *income* between 30 and 40 contacts per day. The reason for this has less to do with the number of contacts being made and more to do with increasing lead follow up calls. **Door knocking puts people into your database.** *Calling them* **converts them to listings.**

Successful agent will tell you that there is a kind of exponential increase in business the more you prospect. You don't merely get twice the results when you double your efforts. You get more than twice the results.

When Will I Get My First Listing?

The average number of doors knocked to get a listing seems to be about 1,200 doors. If you knock 100 doors/day, five days per week, you would reach 1,200 doors in two weeks. However, the number of doors to get a listing is an aggregate over many months. You might have to knock on 2,400 doors before you get a listing, then you suddenly get two listings at once. The average is still 1,200 doors to a listing, but the time took a month instead of two weeks.

Actual results will vary. On the following page are examples from agents answering the question: *How many doors does it take you to get a listing?* These agents are sharing their real numbers over various mastermind forums, illustrating the commonalities of door knocking experiences from different perspectives.

Agent Experiences
How many doors does it take to get a listing?

"I started real estate in 1993. My coach had me knock on 4,000 doors four times a year. I would order 4,000 newsletters and then start knocking on doors. By the time I had finished handing out all the newsletters—only to people I spoke with—I always had 4 listings. I would knock on doors for 3 or 4 days per week in the morning. When I got busy, I'd drop the door knocking. Not clever. A few months down the road, I always regretted it. I can say with certainty that knocking on 1,000 doors, with 1/3 of the people home, will get me a listing."

***

"The weird thing with me right now is I have knocked on over 3,500 doors (attempts) and have no results. Normally for 800 doors I have something. But I've been doing this for three years and I know, when you add them up at the end of the year, the numbers always work out okay in the end. Delayed gratification gone mad. I think the powers that be are just having fun with me right now."

***

"I know an agent who is very secretive about how he works, but he once told me that he had to knock on 1500 doors for a good listing. Another agent, the top door knocker in Toronto once told me 'Anything under 500 people and you're doing good to get a listing.' He recommended that I knock on 2000 -3000 doors a month to get a listing or two each month. I once asked this guy if he was sent to a new city how long it would take him to get a listing. He said, 'Within a week.' Keep in mind this guy was an Olympic athlete for Canada in his younger days."

***

"For every 75 contacts I make, I will get 1 lead (this depends and varies upon turnover/price points/time of year etc.). For every 600 contacts, I

23

will take 1 salable listing. [Author's note: That's about 1800 doors = 1 listing]. I need 6,000 contacts to take 10 listings. I will be following up on 80 leads generated. Based on 200 prospecting days in the year (40 weeks), I need to make 30 contacts per day to take 10 listings per year just from doors."

***

Your numbers will be different, just as these numbers are all different. Yet they're all within a common enough range to justify averaging them out to the figures shown in this guide.

Do these numbers seem daunting?

Let's face it. You have to sift through a lot of chaff to find the heart of the wheat, no matter what form of prospecting you're using. Whether you're calling, knocking, sending mail, meeting at networking events, talking through social media, or buying leads, only about 1 in 1,200 people are planning to move anytime soon. By showing up directly in front of them, you increase the odds that you're the one they'll use when it's time to go.

Is Door Knocking Legal?

Yes, in most communities. Exceptions are planned developments and gated communities that restrict access and specifically post "no soliciting" signs (although there are ways around this, too).

Many cities and townships *officially* require permits for "door-to-door soliciting or canvassing." Some areas provide exceptions for real estate agents. Some don't. Some of these permits are onerous and expensive, which is probably unconstitutional—many such regulations have been struck down as interference with free speech. But who has the time and money to fight city hall?

Below is a sample of the kind of permitting language available on many city websites. Please check your own city for regulations:

Is a commercial solicitation permit required to distribute handbills or advertisements?
A permit is required if a handbill, advertisement or flyer is personally given to a resident. If the handbill, advertisement or flyer is left on the door without contacting the resident, a permit is not required. No handbills or advertisements may be left at a residence which has a "No Soliciting" or "No Trespassing" sign.

Who is considered a non-commercial solicitor?
A non-commercial solicitor is a public entity(schools, government) or a non-profit organization exempt from Federal income tax under 26 U.S.C. 501 (c)(3).

As a non-commercial solicitor, do I need to apply for a permit or register with the City in any manner?
No. Any person, whether volunteer, owner, agent, consignee or employee who is a nonprofit organization exempt from federal income tax under 26 U.S.C 501(c) (3) or a public entity is exempt from soliciting if a residence does not have posted "No Trespassing" or "No Solicitation".

How can I tell if a commercial solicitor is properly permitted?
Each permitted solicitor must carry a copy of the company's permit and have a City issued photo ID badge.

Are newspapers and magazine solicitor's considered commercial solicitors?
No. Solicitation of newspaper and magazine subscriptions is not considered a commercial sale as it is protected by the 1st amendment of the US Constitution. However, they are prohibited from going to a residence if a "No Solicitation" or "No Trespassing" sign is posted.

Does this ordinance pertain to door-to-door solicitations in commercial locations?
No, the ordinance is only applicable to residential solicitation.

All that said, I don't personally know **any** real estate agents who have gotten a permit for door knocking. Most agents either aren't aware of permit requirements in their area, or they decide to brave the streets, sans permit and risk a possible fine. Fines range between $20 and $500, but could be more or less in your area—so check it out if you're concerned.

The vast majority of home owners don't seem to feel disturbed enough by a real estate inquiry to bother complaining. A quick, polite real estate inquiry in most people's eyes is not the same as an aggressive sales pitch from a door-to-door salesperson.

Some neighborhoods get canvassed by solicitors more often than others. In those areas, residents might be more frustrated and quicker to slam the door or complain. But, in 30 years of door knocking, I have never had anyone say to me "Where's your permit?" or call the city to complain. Never. Will it happen to you? I have no idea, but if it worries you, get a permit. Then move on.

In some communities, fake door-to-door solicitors have been used to canvass neighborhoods for committing crimes. Because of that, some neighborhoods might seem more suspicious of door knockers than other neighborhoods. If you sense the area is particularly suspicious, you can talk about it with a few residents and find out if they get a lot of solicitors or have had problems in the past. Then change locations or strategies.

No Soliciting Signs

If an individual resident has posted a "No solicitors" or "No soliciting" sign, then **no one** with or without a permit is allowed to knock on that door for canvassing purposes. However, again, many door knocking agents ignore these signs, as they're often old—left over from previous residents a long time ago. Some of the friendliest people I speak with are behind old "no soliciting" signs. Maybe they never get "hit" by solicitors, so it's a novelty to them.

No Soliciting

If you don't have an appointment or we don't know you – DO NOT disturb us!

- No Charity
- No Food or Menus
- No Home Estimates
- No Petitions
- No Political Causes
- No Religious Appeals
- No Salesman

We don't interrupt your work. Don't interrupt ours!

No Excuses

Do not knock on this door!

I am not recommending *either* that you get a permit or do not get a permit, or that you do or do not knock on doors with "no soliciting" signs. I'm simply telling you what I and other agents do and don't do. Fines for not having a permit if someone decides to take it that far can run between $50 and $500 or more, depending on your area. Investigate your local permit requirements and fines, and make your own decision. The content in this book assumes you have made whatever decision you are comfortable with.

How Do Home Owners React?

The single greatest reason that we resist door knocking is fear of looking rejection in the eye. Of course, in any form of prospecting there is a fear of rejection, but when face-to-face with a live human, we seem to load that rejection with even more meaning.

The truth is, *no* is simply *no*, whether delivered with a quickly closed door, a grumpy noise, or even a cold look. All the emotions we read into it are just that—things we've read into it. Have you ever been in the middle of something—washing the dishes, reading a good book, gardening—and someone knocks on your door? You answer and then feel a small frustration that *this* took you away from what you were doing. You want to get back to what you were doing, so you say, "No, thanks," and shut the door. You've forgotten all about it by the time you get back to what you were doing.

When it comes to the kind of "no's" you'll get, I'm confident the following numbers are generally accurate: Out of 100 contacts, 80 will be considerate—a simple *no* delivered in whatever mood they're in. 17 or so will be extremely nice and chat at length. Maybe two or three people out of 100 will be rude, saying something like "Go away!" or "If I wanted your help I would have asked."

Yet, despite having 98 positive contacts, the 2 negative responses seem to be those we will remember and carry around with us for the next hour, letting them affect our attitude and our *wealth*.

There is an old story about two devout Buddhist monks wandering the land. They came to a river, and beside the river was a beautiful maiden. The monks were forbidden to touch women, but when the maiden cried that she could not cross the river, the older monk

good analogy

unhesitatingly picked her up and carried her across. He set her down and then the monks continued on their way.

Eventually, the older monk noticed the younger seemed tense and angry. "Is something the matter?" he asked. The young monk burst out, *"How could you pick that woman up? You know we are forbidden to touch women!"* The older monk, feeling perfectly at peace, said, *"Yes, but I have left her behind; while you still carry her with you."*

The faster you can let go of the negative energy of the one, the faster you will be able to help the many.

***

The Positive and the Negative
by Mack McCoy, Portland, OR

"The fact of the matter is that [door knocking] is hard work, and the rejections are many and not always polite ... AND if you do it consistently, you will have a successful real estate practice.

For every person or two that feels the need to take the time to let fly at you, there will be many who will be polite, and some number - perhaps it's one in a hundred, maybe one in five hundred, will be glad you knocked because, in fact, they have been thinking of selling and they don't know any real estate agents and, by gosh, you sure seem nice.

Don't let the sad, misanthropic people who have been preparing for the moment that a salesperson rings their phone or knocks on their door discourage you. Normal, healthy people politely ask what the purpose of your visit or call is, and tell you that they are not interested, without making you fear for your safety or your sanitation." [Author—the word *"sanitation"* was used intentionally by Mack.]

***

Overall, most people who answer the door will just be quick—not friendly or unfriendly, but quick to say *"No, thank you."* Or *"No, we're not moving, but thanks for coming by."* Or they'll laugh and say, *"Oh, they'll have to carry me out of here in a box."* Some are extremely nice and will want to talk and talk and talk and then your problem is extracting yourself from the conversation!

For more about dealing with rejection and self-motivation, see **Chapter 4: The Inner Game of Door Knocking**.

Chapter 2:
Door Knocking Strategies

In this chapter, you'll see three different strategies for building listing inventory through door knocking, including:

- Continuous Door Knocking
- Knocking on Purpose
- Farming and Door Knocking

Continuous Door Knocking

Continuous Door Knocking might also be called serial door knocking. Continuous means knocking one street to the next, with no intention of repeating any streets already knocked. This clearly differs from farm door knocking, where the intention is to create relationships and familiarity by doing repeat visits.

Most of the door knocking I've done has been continuous door knocking. I pick a neighborhood I like, drive there, park, get out, go up to the first door and start knocking. Then I continue threading around different blocks until I work my way back to my car. If I haven't hit 100 doors yet, I get in the car and drive to a new area and start again.

Does this work? You bet it does. Unlike farm door knocking, this approach is all about the numbers—hitting as many doors as possible as quickly as possible, looking for the few who are ready to go within the next 12 months or so.

On the following page is an example of how to be successful at continuous door knocking.

The Success of Continuous Door Knocking
by Joe Dalbert, greater Chicago area

I was in an upscale neighborhood I hadn't been in before, so didn't know what to expect yet. So I was surprised when this senior lady answers and says that her son wanted her to move in with him, but she didn't want to. After talking a while, it was clear that she needed to [move in with him], so I set an appointment to meet with her and her son next week and listed the house.

You knock on enough doors and you'll get a few like this. Most of them, you have to keep in touch and then convert them in a few months and sometimes years, if you stay in touch regularly.

***

The keys to successful continuous door knocking are the numbers and the script. Have a solid opening script, a few solid follow-on questions, and a solid closing. Use this sequence over and over. Expect the yeses, maybes, and referrals—be ready for them. Clear the *no's* and find the *yeses.*

Don't plan on returning to houses where no one is home. You'll be knocking on so many doors and moving so fast, that you'll hit far more homes by moving forward than you will by going back and trying to get the homes you missed.

Pros to Continuous Door Knocking:

The clear advantages to serial door knocking include not having to create a neighborhood agent image, not needing to do any specific neighborhood preparation, and not needing to keep track of previous conversations like you do in farming. You can choose to work anywhere you like, in any price point without distraction.

Cons to Continuous Door Knocking:

Since only about 30% of people are home during any one door knocking session, you will miss opportunities by not returning to the same neighborhood at different times of the day. Also, if you enjoy building community you may get bored with serial knocking, as you don't get to build neighborhood visibility and relationships over time, or do any fun farming activities.

If you live in a small town, you may run out of doors to knock on when doing serial door knocking—you can easily knock on 2,000 doors a month doing serial door knocking, so if your area has only 5,000 qualified residences, you'd be done in 2.5 months. Farming strategies will work better in a small town. Finally, occasionally home owners challenge your right to list in their neighborhood because you don't have any track record there—a concern you can address with your overall track record and a good script.

You, here.

Knocking on Purpose

Many agents are more comfortable door knocking when they have a specific purpose in mind. Here are some of the most common reasons that agents use when they are knocking "on purpose:"

Target Properties

Many agents make expireds, fsbo's, and pre-foreclosures/NOD's the center of their door knocking strategy. They plan which homes they want to visit, then they knock on between 20 and 40 doors around their target, including their target. In this way, they kill two birds with one stone—doing continuous door knocking combined with hitting a house where they know there is a need already.

The opening scripts will vary slightly depending on the type of target. For instance, an expired opener might be:

- *"I understand you've been trying to sell your house...You do you still want to sell it, don't you?"*

When opening with a purpose, it's helpful to start with a soft yes/no question, like the previous tag question. (A **tag question** makes a statement, then tags on a question at the end, usually *–don't you?* Or *–do you?*)

I realize there are differences of opinion about using yes/no questions in sales, with many experts preferring to use open-ended questions. But at a cold door, when someone is likely to have their guard up, I don't like starting with an open-ended question that attempts to pry information out of them, such as

- *When do you plan to list your home again?*

- *Why do you think your house didn't sell before?*

Those might be my second questions if they answered affirmatively to my opener.

Another great question format is the **Either/Or**, as in:

> ▪ *"I was wondering, would you like to sell your house now, or will you be listing again with the same agent?*

These are not trick questions. They are smart conversation openers. Learn more about Openers in **Chapter 5: Door Knocking Scripts**.

Looking on Behalf of a Buyer

Using a current buyer as a reason to door knock in a specific neighborhood is a great idea, especially if you're uncomfortable with the whole idea of invading someone's space and asking if they're moving. By saying:

> ▪ *"I have a buyer looking for a home in this neighborhood, and I was wondering..." you are providing a valid reason for being there.*

I use this line when I really do have a buyer looking, and often I'll use a buyer's need to choose which areas I go door knocking. However, I can count on one hand the number of times I've actually put a specific buyer into a house I've found through door knocking. Also, the "I'm looking for a buyer" script takes more time, lowering the number of houses I get through without improving the end results.

Some agents will use this line even if they're not really working with a buyer. Their justification is that as soon as the home is listed, they'll have a buyer. If you feel comfortable doing that, power to you.

Just Listed/Just Sold

Many agents will knock doors around a just listed/just sold. They feel that by announcing the listing or the sale, they're doing a public service and it feels less like selling or asking. If they don't have a listing of their own, they can announce just listeds and just solds all day long for anyone's listing, without permission, as long as they don't claim it was their listing or sold.

The problem for most agents when delivering a just listed/sold script is that they have in mind that they'll be discussing the listing/sold. In fact, that can be a distraction. I like the approach of saying:

- *"We just sold a home around the corner from you and are wondering who else you know who'd like to sell their home." It keeps the focus on lead generation rather than on the sold listing.*

The just listed/just sold door knocking technique is so prevalent that I'll often come across home owners who say, *"You were just here, telling us about that new listing around the corner,"* even though it wasn't me. My favorite come-back line is, *"Oh? What did I tell you?"* Sometimes they laugh and say, *"Well, I guess it wasn't you, but..."*

***

Just Listed Door Knocking
by Julie Antunes, Southeby's, Cave Creek, AZ

"I've experienced door knocking can be worthwhile very recently. I listed a condo and had a postcard made up with the listing information and a photo of the home. Instead of doing the typical mailing, I went knocking on doors in the community where I listed it.

I wanted to let the owners in the complex know about the new listing and figured I'd probably leave the majority of postcards in the doorway when no one answered. To my surprise, more than half of the residents answered the door in this seasonal, mostly retired community.

Not only did I get to pass out business cards and make a connection with many owners, I actually got another listing! Several others said they were thinking about listing and now that they met me, would be in touch when the time came.

Of course, you have to know the population type in the area you are targeting to hopefully get owners at home. In this case, I went during the weekday morning before people left for daytime golf or other activities. If you don't have a listing in the area you wish to market, do a marketing piece on a new listing and use that one as your 'door opener' when going around."

***

Open House Invitations

Some agents will door knock around open houses, to invite neighboring home owners to drop by. If you want to demonstrate your effectiveness, inviting neighboring home owners to your open houses shows them you're friendly, professional, and industrious. Many home owners tell me they selected their real estate agent by going to nearby open houses in their community.

On the next page is an example of one of the simple, "homespun" flyers I use. This home was purchased and remodeled, and the neighbors were curious.

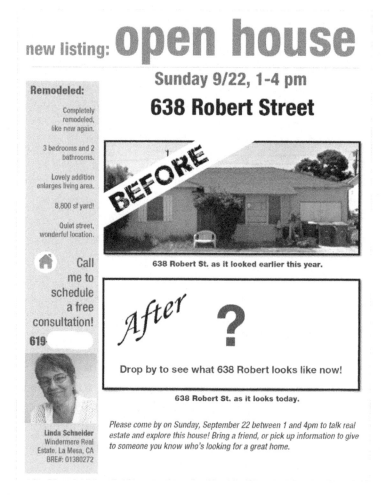

new listing: open house

Sunday 9/22, 1-4 pm

638 Robert Street

Remodeled:

Completely remodeled, like new again.

3 bedrooms and 2 bathrooms.

Lovely addition enlarges living area.

8,800 sf yard!

Quiet street, wonderful location.

Call me to schedule a free consultation!

619-

Linda Schneider
Windermere Real Estate, La Mesa, CA
BRE#: 01380272

BEFORE

638 Robert St. as it looked earlier this year.

After **?**

Drop by to see what 638 Robert looks like now!

638 Robert St. as it looks today.

Please come by on Sunday, September 22 between 1 and 4pm to talk real estate and explore this house! Bring a friend, or pick up information to give to someone you know who's looking for a great home.

Pros to Knocking on Purpose:

Agents can double up on their efforts—both knocking on doors in the general sense and addressing a specific property. Having a purpose makes agents comfortable about knocking. In areas where soliciting is not allowed, presenting an invitation to an open house or announcing a just listed may be acceptable, as you are not soliciting for business specifically.

Cons to Knocking on Purpose:

Many agents waste time driving to different areas and knocking too few doors. Others only door knock when they feel they have a purpose, and they abandon door knocking at other times. And finally, agents knocking on purpose tend to over-focus on the targeted property or reason for being there, and forget to ask about moving plans.

Interview with a Door Knocking Powerhouse

Following is a brief interview with Froy Candelario, a real estate agent in the Los Angeles area who started door knocking in the mid-1980's after attending a Mike Ferry seminar.

Mr. Candelario is gregarious, multi-million dollar producing real estate agent with a near-legendary real estate volume almost entirely within the Hispanic community of L.A. Licensed in 1984, Froy started his business with nothing but a fanatical work ethic and the advice to go door knocking. He continued knocking for almost 20 years, before shifting his business recently to a phone-based real estate practice. Froy has much to teach us about the art of door knocking. This is an excerpt from an interview I conducted with him over the phone in September, 2013. Note that Froy's first language is not English.

***

Interview with Froy Candelario
Superstar Realty/My Real Estate Plaza

What was your typical day of door knocking like?

Number one, you got to get up early. I got up at 3:30 in the morning to go to the gym to make sure that I was ready physically. I took my shower and got dressed for the day in the gym. Then at 8:00 I was at the doors, at eight sharp. I started then and I went to 11:45.

I had lunch all the way to 1:30, then doors again all the way to 4:00. From 4:00 to 6:00 or so I had the appointments. The assistant would call me if I had appointments and if I didn't have any appointments, then I would stay door knocking until late. But most likely I would have appointments at the office and take two or three listings every day. My staff runs through the listing information and then I meet the client and they sign the listing agreement.

When you were at the doors, what were you doing and saying?

I had a lot of fun. Far away from the door, before I got to the door, I yelled, "Well, good morning," and things like that. "Hi, good morning." Screaming and yelling…and obviously at that time of the morning people wondered who was yelling like that. The dogs were barking left and right and so by the time I got to the door they were already there, and a lot of times I didn't even have to knock.

Then the first thing I said was, "You know, we're selling a house close to yours right here around the corner. Who do you know who is looking to buy a house?" Always. Now, there are two things that happen right then. There is the way you deliver that message, and also the energy that you put into the door. I notice the energy, because I sometimes had someone door knocking with me, I noticed they didn't have energy, and they didn't believe what they were saying.

Then I asked when they are thinking of moving and they would say, "I was thinking…" That was the key, when they said "I was thinking…" then I would just go on and follow the script. I used the Mike Ferry scripts, or some like that. If they said they were thinking about it, then it was done. Even if it was six months from now or seven months from now, or a year, they were mine. I believed that.

What did you do to keep in touch with people who were moving in seven months or a year?

What I did was set an appointment. Always an appointment. When they said, "Yes I'm thinking about it six months from now," I said, "Okay then, I'm planning on meeting you six months from now. I'll be calling you." Who did follow-up was my assistant. She would say, "Mr. Smith, you have an appointment with Mr. Candelario seven months from now. We want to make sure you are okay with that?" Then she would call and remind them of the appointment in six months and then just before. They would be there or they would cancel. My job was to set appointments.

What advice would you give to somebody who would like to succeed at door-to-door prospecting?

Number one, you got to believe in yourself. Have the right attitude and the right energy. You will find that the majority of people have no interest. You're not looking for them, you're looking for those who are interested. That's why you're asking a question. When you ask the question, it has to be so positive and you have to believe in the question, so you have that energy coming from within.

If you come with the wrong energy, or you're hinting, saying "Do you think maybe...?" No! You have to say, "When are you planning on moving? Have you ever thought of buying a house?" You have to always to be very, very, very SURE that this is what you want to say. Energy is everything. You can actually invite them with your energy.

***

Not everyone can do doors the way Froy does doors. Still, when you get advice from a master, you at least try. So after this interview, I decided to try calling out loudly as I came up to the doors. "Hello, it's Linda!" They didn't know me, but I thought that by using my name, they would be curious, and they generally were.

When I was calling through a screen door, people would call back to me, "yes?" When the door was shut, I don't know if they could hear me inside, but when they answered the door, they also seemed curious and friendly. I don't believe the yelling ahead made any difference in my results, but it did seem to put people more at ease, perhaps because I'm not surprising them. Most importantly, it raised my energy, so that my come-from was very enthusiastic. I was inviting them with my energy.

Farming and Door Knocking

The vast majority of door knocking real estate agents do it within the context of a geographic farm.

The farming analogy, of course, refers to how a farmer prepares the soil, sows the seeds, fertilizes and nurtures the seeds as they grow, and eventually harvests the crop. In the case of geographic farming, the soil and the seeds are your contacts and connections within a neighborhood, and you harvest good listings and buyers. Contrast this with continuous door knocking, which is more akin to hunting than farming.

Geographic farming is also known as *building a listing bank*, *neighborhood marketing*, *or being a neighborhood expert*.

Farming can include a tremendous variety of communication strategies, all designed to keep your name and face top of mind for people in the community. Farming tactics can include hand-delivering flyers, giving away *tchotchka* (a Yiddish word meaning an inexpensive trinket), doing mailings, networking at neighborhood events, sponsoring local teams, sponsoring garage sales, dropping by random weekend garage sales, advertising in local papers, running bus bench ads, creating a neighborhood newsletter, placing little flags on the lawn on Independence Day, delivering seeds in the Spring, and so much more, limited only by time, money, and imagination.

Door knocking is like the icing on the cake of farming. All the marketing you do is designed to show you're an expert and to keep your name top of mind. But it's your face-to-face real estate conversations that will truly cement you in their minds as the person to call.

When farming, plan to knock the entire farm **every six to twelve weeks**. Door knocking makes you visible to people. Your goal in farm door knocking is to have great conversations and position yourself as the obvious expert over time.

***

Mini-Farm Door Knocking Success
with R.B. (AKA Arby), San Diego

R.B., formerly with One Source Realty in San Diego, California, used a simple micro farming strategy to become rookie of the year in 2005.

Soon after getting her real estate license, R.B. started door knocking a neighborhood of just under 800 homes repeatedly. She started at one end of the neighborhood and when she got to the other end, she started over again. She knocked at different times of the day so she'd reach people at home at different times.

If she spoke to the same person repeatedly, she let them know she was just checking in with them, updating them on what was happening in the real estate market. If someone had already been rude to her, she skipped that door next time. She hand-delivered a market update flyer on each round, but did no other marketing.

Her script at first was a general door knocking script, but as she gained listings and sales, it became more of a just listed/sold script.

Within one year, she had gained a whopping 14% of listings in that neighborhood. However, 14% was only five listings. Was it worth it? It was when you consider that the average price in the neighborhood was $600,000 and R.B. was able to parlay those listings into 12 deals for the year—and a $126,000 income for her first year in business.

***

Another agent loved doing giveaways with farming. She had a neighborhood of about 1,500 homes and went by every month. She always took something to hand out—seeds in the spring, calendars at Christmas, newsletters, note pads, pumpkins at Halloween, etc. She made a great income, but had to invest quite a bit of money. Would she have done just as well without all the *tchotchka*? We'll never know. She did it that way because she loved doing it that way.

The point is that you can farm with or without expensive giveaways or sponsorships, if you door knock there regularly.

What Is the Ideal Farm Size?

A good sized farm for door knocking is between 1,200 and 3,000 homes. However, there is wide disagreement about ideal farm size. I've chosen this size range based on door knocking reach.

Suppose an agent picks a 3,000-door farm. If that agent knocked just 4 days a week, he would be through the entire area in just 7.5 weeks.

If the agent cut back to 3 days a week of door knocking, he could maintain a comfortable 10 week rotation through the farm. That's 5 visits a year...plenty to maintain top of mind presence.

But the size of the farm isn't as important as the number of sales there. If there are enough sales in a 1,500-home farm to achieve your financial goals, then you don't need a larger farm. If there are not enough sales to reach your financial goals, then you need a larger farm, an area with higher turnover, or more than one farm.

How to Identify a Good Farm

To find a farm and determine if it will fulfill your financial goals, take the following steps:

1. Look for an area you like working and establish the boundaries of what you consider to be the farm. That's the fun part.

2. Go into your MLS and find the **number of listings** for the most recent 12-month period within those street boundaries. Also look at the **agent names**. If any one agent seems to have the lion's share of listings, you may not want to compete head-to-head with them. But that doesn't mean you can't make headway over time. Some home owners want an alternative.

3. Go to a database like corelogic.com, or work with your title rep to get a **total number of homes** in the area you've selected.

4. Divide #2 (total listings) by #3 (total homes) to get a turnover rate. Ideally, a farm will have a 4% + turnover rate, and a well-established listing agent will capture 8% - 15% of those listings.

Example:

- *179 (#listings) ÷ 4,388 (#residences) = .04 (4% turnover rate)*

- *Agent captures 8% of 179 listings = 14 listings*

Let's look at an example in real life:

A high-producing agent in San Diego, has worked a mid to high-priced neighborhood of San Diego called Talmadge for around 20 years. Talmadge has 1,990 properties.

Over a 12 month period (at this writing) there were 138 listings there—a turnover rate of 6.9%. The agent took 15 of those listings, which is a 10.9% capture rate (15/138). She also works a second neighborhood with similar demographics and numbers, and has a very active referral base. That means she is generating around 30 listings per year, and probably 60 transactions from doors and referrals together. Her price point averages around $550,000. You do the math and it equals a lot of money no matter what sort of split she's on.

***

Welcome Wagon Approach

I (the author) bought a FSBO in Talmadge in 2005. Soon after moving in, I got a knock at the door. It was this same agent, intending to welcome the newcomers to the neighborhood and incidentally start a relationship with them. Since we worked at the same office at the time, it was a bit of a surprise to both of us when I answered the door, and we had a good laugh. But it also gave me insight into one of her farming techniques. Since then, I have met other agents who style themselves as the unofficial, old-school "welcome wagon" for their neighborhoods, greeting all new residents, whether or not the agent represented them.

We all know that agents more often lose track of their clients after closing than not. So this is an excellent strategy for capturing "orphan" clients.

***

Pros to Farm Door Knocking:

Agents get to know the community intimately, which helps them find opportunities and build credibility. Home owners trust agents they've seen numerous times. Agents eventually get to talk to most of home owners by going back to doors at different times on different days. Agents double up on their visibility through advertising and marketing in addition to door knocking.

Finally, agents who enjoy building community can sponsor groups and activities. For instance, one agent outside of Vancouver has started a book reading group, a Bunko group, and a Friday night kid's fun group in her neighborhood.

Cons to Farm Door Knocking:

There are *not* a lot of negatives to farming. In fact, I can think of only two reasons to consider other door knocking strategies: First, if you're not a highly social or organized person, continuous door knocking might be more appealing than putting together marketing plans, socializing, dropping by garage sales, etc.

Second, by door knocking in the same group of houses over and over again, agents lower the odds of finding new listing opportunities, until they build up enough credibility and momentum. It can take two years or more to start capturing 8% to 15% of a farm's listings, which means a long lag time during which you'll be lighter on listings that you might want to be.

Combining Direct Mail and Farming

I'm not a fan of direct mail as a core prospecting strategy unless you have a steady flow of money and can afford it. Of course, it's a strategy that works and can be highly profitable, but it is very expensive, especially if you're an agent trying to bootstrap your business on limited resources.

Mail must be sent at least 6 times a year to do any good. Suppose you mail to 1,000 addresses and garner a 1.5% response rate. Over the year, you will have 15 people rise to your call to action. About 10% of them will list with you. That's one listing for a cost of around $2,700. Now, I agree that in some high-priced areas, that's not a bad return...if you're making a commission of $30,000, that's a 9% cost. But if you're making a $5,000 commission, it's a 54% cost.

However, there are a couple of ways to combine farming and direct mail to increase the return on your investment in direct mail.

For instance, you can mail to a sub-set or core of homes within your farm. By mailing to 500 for every 1,000 doors in your farm, and only mailing 4 times a year, you significantly reduce your mailing costs. You can only do this because you are already door knocking in the area. Since neighbors sometimes talk to neighbors, your mailings might be passed along to those who don't get them regularly.

***

Farming & Direct Mail Technique

Many years ago a now prominent Seattle broker couldn't afford direct mail, so he targeted just 50 homes for mailing. But he didn't pick 50 homes in a solid block. Instead, he targeted 50 homes sprinkled throughout an area he wanted to farm. Those 50 homes were owned by his ideal market—seniors who would be downsizing soon. He then door knocked the neighborhood around those 50 homes. The result was that he appeared bigger than he really was. He was able to list three of those 50 homes in his first year. By his second year, he had expanded his mailing program to 300 homes.

***

Also, instead of paying postage, you can hand-deliver your direct response mail in the form of a flyer or newsletter. When you are hand delivering direct response "mail," don't mix it up with your door knocking. It might be better to have a high-school or college kid deliver your piece while you continue door knocking. (See the FAQ **What Should I Hand Out?** for more information.)

Direct Mail Content Ideas

What kinds of things should you deliver in your direct mail? Here are a few direct response mail ideas. Keep in mind that it's not direct RESPONSE unless you include a call to action...something that gets them to respond.

1. Just Listed/Sold Postcards: These postcards show properties that have just been listed or sold by you or someone in your company. You can add a small list of other homes that have been listed or sold recently. A call to action might be *Call to Find Out What Your Home Is Worth Today!* Following is an example of how simple and un-flashy these postcards can be, yet still get plenty of attention.

2. Proof of Success Postcards: Do you have great stories about how you've helped past clients? Tell each story in a short paragraph, put it on a postcard, and mail it once a month. People love stories, and if you can include a small picture of the person you helped, you'll increase the social connection you make. A call to action might be related to the content of your story. Following is an example of how simple this card can be...**the *low resolution* of this image was the best this agent was able to send for publication!**

3. **Annual Schedule Postcards or Flyers:** These are the kind of things people hang onto and post on the 'fridge or a bulletin board. They contain information like National Park schedules, football team schedules, farmer's market schedules, list of local bed and breakfasts, things to do in the area, etc.

These postcards have a long shelf life and can bring you a lot of future business. These are not really direct response mail, since there isn't really a reason for people to call you. But they should display your contact information and face.

4. Special Offer Postcards or Flyers: This is a way to offer your prospects a free ebook, free market analysis, free list of foreclosures, free in-home staging consultation, etc. FREE is a key word, and the call to action is obvious. Below is an example of a co-branded postcard sent on behalf of a carpet cleaner to the Realtor's list. The carpet cleaner returns the favor by sending a "deal" from the Realtor to his carpet customer list.

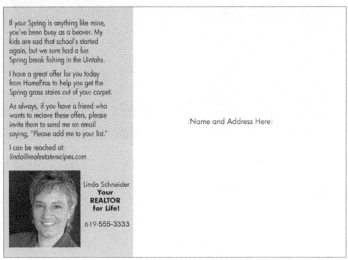

5. Event Announcement Postcards: Know of an upcoming opening, a new play, a special deal for an area restaurant? Work with the organization to create and send dual-purpose postcard announcements.

Planning a neighborhood garage sale? Organize your team to go door to door, or just mail postcards!

Or create open house invitations and mail these as event announcements. The call to action might be more oblique, like *Call and let me know how you liked the restaurant.*

6. Direct Response Newsletters: Use entertainment to capture and keep attention over time. Interspersed with the content, include calls to action of different kinds. Include contests, quizzes, free reports, invitations to get information, etc. But remember that the most important ingredients in direct mail marketing are repetition and longevity—giving people a reason to see you repeatedly. Below is an example of the first page of a newsletter that contains numerous calls to action, mixed with entertaining information. (See **www.FastNewsletters.com**.)

January 2014   by Jason Wright ● 555-333-2222

front porch news

Need help around the house?

Call me when you need a referral to a great handyman, plumber, painter, electrician, etc!

555-333-2222

Why piggy banks?

Dogs bury bones. Squirrels gather nuts. Camels store food and water. But what do pig save? Nothing! They bury nothing, store nothing, and save nothing.

So why do we save our coins in a piggy bank? During The Middle Ages, in about the fifteenth century, metal was expensive and seldom used for household wares. Instead, dishes and pots were made of "pygg," a cheap type of clay used for making household objects. People often saved money in kitchen jars made of pygg, called "pygg jars." When housewives could save an extra coin, they dropped it into a clay jars. They called it their pygg bank.

Over the next two hundred to three hundred years, people forgot that "pygg" referred to the earthenware material. Gradually the word was perverted to "piggy." In the nineteenth century when English potters received requests for piggy banks, they produced banks shaped like a pig.

Spontaneous living room games for winter

Your Home—Parents, grandparents, and babysitters are always looking for easy ways to entertain the kids. Here are 6 spontaneous games you can play on the spur of the moment, with no preparation or props:

Question game: Have a conversation using only questions. Statements and repetitions not allowed!

The story game: Start a made-up story, pass it around, allowing each person to add their own twist to it.

Telephone: Whisper a phrase in a person's ear, then they whisper it in the next person's ear, and so on. The last person says it out loud.

Haywire compass: Invite kids to stand in middle of room, close eyes, point with arm out, then spin. When stopped, they guess what they're pointing at.

Outrageous Exercise: Challenge one another to do funny exercises, like sticking out tongue 20 times.

From Spontaneous Family Games on Amazon Kindle ($2.99)

Wondering what your home is worth today?

If you're curious about your home's value these days, I can easily give you an estimate. Give me a call at 555-333-2222 or send me an email GreatestAgent@greatestcompany.com and I'll get that information to you.

Chapter 3:
Harvesting Leads

When you're in the trenches doing door knocking, you'll get many different responses, leading to many script options. Knowing how to direct the conversation and secure the next step in each situation is useful in nurturing a variety of lead types.

What kinds of leads will you come across in your door knocking, and what do you need to know about them? Which leads are worth pursuing and which are a waste of time? It won't take you long to develop a sense of leads. But to give you a leg up and answer some of the questions you might be wondering about, here's a primer on door knocking leads, covering the following topics:

- What Counts as a Lead in Door Knocking?
- Examples of Listings Taken Through Door Knocking
- Fake Leads
- On a Typical Day of Door Knocking
- Keeping Score and Tracking Results

What Counts as a Lead in Door Knocking?

A door knocking lead is generally one of three things:

- **Hot Lead:** Owner is committed to selling within the next few weeks or months.
- **Warm Lead:** Owner has an 80% or better chance of selling in the next two years.
- **Possible Lead:** Possibility of being hot, warm, or nothing—the situation requires further investigation. It could be a vacant home, a referral from a neighbor, a house that's being painted, and so on.

A hot lead is one where the owner says, *"Why, yes. I am thinking about moving. I've just called a Realtor to talk about listing. Would you like to tell us what you would do to sell our house?"* You must be ready for that, because it will happen, and it is likely to take you completely by surprise.

Hot leads might be as straight-forward as that, or might be more circumspect, as in *"Well, there's a possibility of my husband getting a job offer in June. If that happened we'd probably move in July."* What this person is saying is *"Yes."* Treat it as a hot lead. Rehearse your responses. See **Chapter 5: Door Knocking Scripts**.

Warm leads are leads where the owner has told you they will be moving in the future—within a specific time frame, but they're really just thinking about it, with no definite plans. For instance, *"Yeah, we might move next June when my daughter graduates from college, but it could still be a year or two. We're not sure."* This lead can be converted in time by following up fanatically. If they do decide to move, you want to be the one they trust with the listing. (See Chapter 6, **Fanatical Follow Up** for more about converting warm leads.)

Possible leads are first steps only, and not really leads at all. Before you count this type as a lead, you need to do more digging. For instance, if the neighbor says a rental across the street is going to be put up for sale, you have a *possible lead.* Now you must call the owner of the rental. If the owner tells you she is planning to sell next month, then you have a hot lead.

But if the owner says she's not selling, and *"Who in the blankty-blank gave you that information?!"*, then it was never a lead in the first place, and wouldn't be counted as such in the final numbers. It was just a *possibility that didn't pan out.* If you track possible leads, see how often they convert to warm or hot leads, then you will have a measure and can tell in a few weeks if you're wasting too much time on possibilities that don't pan out.

How much research should you do to find out if a *possible lead* is real or not? That's up to you, and probably related to the situation. If it's a vacant home that the neighbors tell you has been vacant for ten years, you probably would be wasting your time to follow up. The owner is completely unmotivated to sell and probably many other agents have already tried. On the other hand, if the neighbors tell you a home has been vacant for three weeks since the tenants moved out, it might be worth pursuing. Maybe the owner is having trouble renting it and it's time to sell?

Sometimes you can't dig up a phone number for the owner. If you have a boilerplate letter available for this type of situation, then pop it in the mail and send it to the owner's address of record, then forget about it. If the owner contacts you, wonderful. Otherwise, drop it. Don't count it as a lead until you speak to the owner and can re-categorize it as hot or warm.

Examples of Listings Taken through Door Knocking

Listing leads can look like many different things in real estate, especially in door knocking. Here are a few examples of real listings taken from door knocking:

Perfectly Timed Listing: Hot leads are a matter of being in the right place at the right time. For instance, I knocked on the door of a mini-dorm in our college area. The student who answered told me his father, who lived out of the area, owned the home, and was in the process of selling the house. He thought it was already listed but wasn't sure. He got his father on the phone for me. Father told me he was about to sign the paperwork for an agent his son had selected based on seeing signs in the area of the house. Dad and son were willing to list with me as I was clearly a hard working (and convincing) agent. I sent the paperwork and called Dad to make sure he signed it.

Even if I had not gotten the listing, I would have counted it in my stats as a hot lead. Why count leads you don't land? Because when you're finished with several weeks and months of door knocking, you want to be able to review your stats. From that information you will know how many doors you must knock on to get lead, and how many leads turn into listings. If you're getting a lot of leads but no listings, then you need to work on your conversion skills, or re-evaluate what you're counting as a lead. (See Fake Leads below.)

Death in the Family Listing: This is a very common lead type. It's usually a neighbor giving you the heads up through neighborhood gossip. Sometimes the neighbor has a phone number or name and you can track down the heirs. Sometimes you have to resort to creativity. The first time I came across one of these leads, the neighbor told me the heirs were in town, trying deciding what to do with it. She did not know how to reach them. I tried several other neighbors with no luck, but they had no further information.

I went back to the office, printed up a letter about how I would love to represent them. I put it and my **pre-listing package** into a Fed-Ex envelope. On the outside of the envelope I hand-wrote a brief note telling them that the neighbors had suggested I get in touch and inside was real estate information to open right away. Then I drove back to the house, dropped it on the doorstep, and returned to door knocking. Within 30 minutes, I got a call from the heirs wanting to set an appointment to meet me that afternoon, at which time I listed the house on the spot. This is also an example of a perfectly timed lead.

Other *death in the family leads* are harder to track down. If the neighbors can't help you, and public records only show the previous (now deceased) owners, you might be left with sending a letter and then forgetting about it, just as with any vacant home lead.

Vacant Home Listing: I'm always surprised by how many homes are vacant—even in the nicest of neighborhoods. The first time I found a listing this way, I was in a pristine area with manicured lawns and BMW's in the drives. None of the neighbors knew the home was vacant. A gardener was maintaining the home. When I got in touch with the owner, it turned out that he had relocated for a job, but thought the market wasn't ripe yet for selling. I converted him to a warm lead and stayed with him. He listed within six months.

I once listed a vacant house from someone who was in jail. The neighbors told me the owner was in jail, so I contacted the jail and set up a meeting with him. I got his signature on the listing and conducted the sale entirely behind bars! He still had a legal right to sell his home.

Not all vacant houses are leads. I've seen many unkempt eyesores that the neighbors would love to see sold. But the current owner is either unstable or sentimental, or has other odd reasons to retain the home. If the owner doesn't want to sell, it's not a lead.

Other Possibilities to Keep Your Eye On

Other lead possibilities might be less obvious, but are still very common. For instance, you will notice **a house being cleaned or painted**, which is a sign that someone is possibly fixing up to sell. You will **get referrals** from people who mention someone else is thinking of moving. You will come across **renters** who might want to be buyers.

Fake Leads

With the huge variety of situations that could turn out to be leads, it's possible to run across situations that seem like leads, but are not really. In the following situations, none of these home owners have any motivation to move:

1. Someone says they'd sell if the price were right. *The price is never going to be right.*
2. Someone has been thinking about moving to _____ for the past 12 years. *They'll never move.*
3. Someone wishes they could afford to live closer to the ocean if I could find them a "deal." *They'll never be able to afford it — and besides, when I have that kind of deal, I work with one of my loyal clients who pays cash.*
4. Someone wonders what their house is worth, but otherwise they don't pass any of your qualifying questions. *They're just curious — refer them to Zillow.*

Fake leads waste time. Become ruthless about recognizing them early and removing yourself from the conversation as quickly as possible.

On a Typical Day of Door Knocking

In any one day of door knocking, you can expect one to three *hot or warm leads,* and two to three *possibilities.* To illustrate, here's an account of a door knocking contest that I had with a door knocking partner:

***

The Partner Contest
with Linda Schneider and Lori Martinez, San Diego

On this day, Lori took one side of the street and I took the other. We decided to make a contest of it to see who could come up with the most leads and appointments.

I knocked on 27 doors and spoke to six people before a neighbor told me about the owner of the rental next door wanted to sell. The neighbor didn't want to give me his phone number, but took my card and promised to pass it along. I asked several more neighbors if they had his phone number, but *no one did. I didn't want to ask the tenants (a quick way to anger the owner of a rental). Once back at my office, I would look up the owner in public records and send him my standard letter for these types of leads. Score one **possible** lead.*

*A few doors further along was a woman who wanted to move to a more kid-friendly neighborhood. She and her husband didn't know how to go about selling then buying again. They weren't highly motivated, but definitely interested. There are many sellers like this—frozen in indecision so they do nothing. After some conversation, I decided there was at least an 80% chance that they would move in the next one to two years. They would go into my high-touch automatic follow-up system to build credibility and recognition. Score one **warm** lead.*

*About 30 doors later, a man said he'd love to sell but he's upside down in his mortgage and figured he was stuck there another year or two. I asked how he knew he was upside down, and he said he was guessing. After some discussion and a tour of his home, I could tell that he didn't know how much home values had risen in his area. Back at the office, we would run a CMA, get his current mortgage information, and provide him with a net sheet based on today's values. Score a **warm** lead, but if the value is there, it might turn **hot**.*

*On the last door of the day, I spoke to a nice man who said he wasn't moving. At the same time, he seemed to want to keep talking about the real estate market. After a bit more chatting, he said he had a condo that was, as he put it, "a pain in the rear." He had to evict his tenant and the tenant was resisting. He wondered what the condo was worth and if he could sell it if the tenant was still in the unit. We set a listing appointment on the spot. Score one **hot** lead.*

*My score for the day was **91 doors, 27 contacts, 4 leads (1 possible, 2 warm, and 1 hot)**. Lori's stats were **112 doors, 32 contacts, 4 leads (2 possible and 2 warm)**. Although we got the same number of leads, my hot lead counted for more than one of her possible leads, so I won!*

Keeping Score and Tracking Results

Professional agents track their numbers. They can tell you how many doors they have to knock on to get how many leads to get how many listings to get how much income.

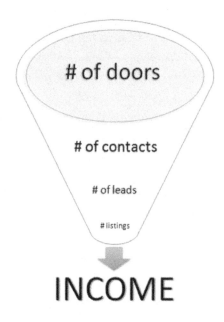

The more in at the top,
the more out the bottom.

To keep track of your results when door knocking, there are different techniques. Some agents will use a clicker and click it for each door they knock (I tried this, but kept forgetting if I'd already clicked or not).

Some will count the doors in the neighborhood ahead of time, then go knocking, knowing that when they're done, they knocked on this many doors.

Some, like Froy Candelario, will print 100 flyers and when they're done passing them out, they know they've knocked on 100 doors.

I've used this approach, and it works well, except that I get tired of holding the flyers and occasionally drop them.

I prefer to keep score by a simple system of marks on my clipboard or notepad, and even sometimes on the back of a business card. I use hash marks, circles and checks—hash marks for every door I knock, circled if I speak to someone at that door, checked if they are a lead:

This allows me to see at a glance how I'm doing. Below is a snapshot of my notebook, showing you how that looks in practice:

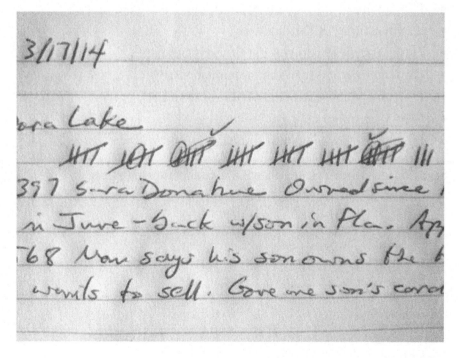

At a glance, I can see that I knocked on 38 doors,
made 5 contacts, and got 2 leads.

I keep notes about the conversation. I also write the names, addresses, and emails of people I speak to length, *even if they're not a lead.* I ask if I can follow up with them, then I send them a handwritten thank you note and add them to my C-level automatic follow up system. Once they're in my automatic follow up system, it takes no effort to keep in touch.

You'll develop your own system for keeping score. Do what works best for you.

The important thing is that you are able after a few weeks or months to provide the following predictive data:

- How many doors do you knock in an hour?
- How many people are generally home when you knock?
- At what times of the day?
- How many leads do you get (of each type)?
- How many leads turn into appointments?
- How many appointments turn into listings?
- How many doors do you knock to get a listing?
- How many hours of door knocking will result in a listing?

Such data will provide you with a road map for success.

Chapter 4:
The Inner Game of Door Knocking

Door knocking requires determination in the face of social awkwardness. Most of us have been taught that it's impolite to ask for something from strangers, it's rude to invade someone's personal space, and that we are being prideful and arrogant if we promote ourselves. No wonder so many real estate agents struggle with prospecting.

Door knocking feels like *selling* to many agents. But no matter what you believe about selling, you can't deny that skilled salespeople have more influence and make more money than unskilled salespeople. They're better at asking for and getting referrals, better at converting leads, and better at engaging with strangers.

I was leading a seminar for By Referral Only in Utah one year. While at lunch, I was challenged about something we had been discussing during the session. I asserted that, if done correctly, you could ask for a referral from even a complete stranger. So to make my point, I volunteered to ask the waitress for a referral.

When the waitress took our order, I asked how long she'd worked at the restaurant and did she like the work she was doing. Then I explained that we were Realtors in town for a workshop. We chatted for a few more minutes while she waited on our table. Finally, I asked if she knew anyone who was thinking about buying a house. She said that her boyfriend was thinking about it. I asked if she would be willing to contact him and introduce him to one of the Realtors at the table. She used that agent's phone, gave her boyfriend the story, and then handed the phone back to the agent. They set an appointment on the spot.

Does the thought of doing that make you cringe? Do you consider it to be rude or inappropriate, or downright embarrassing to ask questions of strangers?

Or are you wondering why you never thought of it before?

With the right energy and the right language, you can create a dynamic with almost anyone that allows you to ask for business, even from a perfect stranger. I didn't simply "chat" with the waitress. I chatted in such a way that positioned me to ask for the referral.

In sales, we must be forward. We must make the first move. We must shoulder the burden of feeling awkward. We must be the ones to risk rejection. *What if they say no? It would be so embarrassing! I'll probably botch it and they'll say no anyway, so why bother? I couldn't stand the embarrassment.*

Feelings of awkwardness and pessimism often lead to "prospecting reluctance," or "fear of prospecting," terms that refer to our wanting to avoid the feeling associated with prospecting. It's a visceral sensation that many of us literally feel in our guts.

If you suffer from prospecting reluctance, there are a number of solutions that can help you overcome it—at least enough so that it doesn't interfere with your success. Always the first solution to try is: Just get started. Once started, the reluctance usually fades quickly. If you dwell on it, getting started just gets harder. The hardest door to get past in door knocking is your own front door.

Think of it like jumping into a cold swimming pool. Everyone knows it's better to jump in and get the shock over with all at once. But a bunch of us prefer to take it slow, working up our nerve to go in just a bit, then working up our nerve again to go in just a bit further, and so on. Each little shock of cold water that goes a bit higher on our bellies makes us want to quit all over again. Often we get only so far, and then we quit, preferring to sit it out while others splash and play.

Getting started with door knocking is best done quickly. Jump right in and get the shock over with. As soon as you do, you'll find yourself enjoying it rather than sitting out watching others make money.

If that solution doesn't work, there are other solutions to try. After all, prospecting reluctance comes in many forms, causing even the most determined agents to prefer cleaning the toilet instead of prospecting.

For you perfectly normal agents who are reluctant to get started, the remainder of this chapter is devoted to techniques you can use to bolster your inner game of prospecting. **Some of these reluctance-blasting techniques will be effective for you; some won't, depending on your nature and the type of reluctance you experience.** Read through each technique and try them all. You may find something here that makes a dramatic difference.

By the way, there is no substitute for a good motivational coach to hold you accountable to a prospecting program. If you're like other real estate agents, you struggle through periods of disorganization and inability to hold yourself to task. A good coach has unique skills for helping you accomplish more. They're not just other real estate agents telling you what works — they're professional real estate business coaches who understand how to psychologically motivate you and find your best opportunities for growth, then help you design a plan and stick to it. What would your business be like if you had a coach like that? Expect to pay a coach $300 to $700/month. As a result, you will make at least twice as much as would have without the coach.

Reluctance-Blasting Techniques

Technique 1: Set Action-Based Goals

When you're crystal clear about how much money you need and what that money will mean to you in terms of *real things* (paying for the kids' braces, owning a wonderful house, helping others in need, etc.) you find it easier to get moving.

Be specific. When setting goals, think beyond the thing you want. Add the reasons that you want it. Then work backwards from your goal to specific actions. For example:

- **Goal:** *I want a 5 bedroom house in North Park with an ocean view.* **Why?** *It will be a home where we put down roots and stay for the next 20 years. A home we can pass on to the kids. Our security.*
- **Timeframe:** *By August of XXXX year (19 months).*
- **High-level objective:** *I will save $70,000 between now and then.*
- **Intermediate objective 1: (Use as many intermediate objectives as necessary.)** *I will maintain an income of $8,000/month between now and then, so I can put aside $3,700/month.*
- **Intermediate objective 2:** *I will close 2 transactions per month.*

- **Intermediate objective 3:** *I will sell my Porsche and save $500/month.*
- **Detailed actions:** 1) Hold two open houses/week. 2) Knock on 500 doors/week and call 40 people/week. 3) Send my newsletter monthly. 4) Call my A level people and ask for a *referral wheel* appointment.

To establish the right actions, use a business plan to identify the specific activities that will give you the results you seek. You can get a copy of my business planning tool through Fiverr.com: **http://fiverr.com/accomplishtrain/provide-real-estate-business-analysis-plan-template**, or you can check with your broker for one.

Technique 2: Follow the 90-Day Rule

There's a great expression in real estate sales: **If you want to know how you did today, check your bank balance in 90 days.** Every time you're tempted to take an extra long lunch or waste time perfecting another real estate flyer, ask yourself what results *this moment* will show up as in 90 days. Try to force yourself into meaningful activities that have concrete results. I have a sign in my office that says:

How Will <u>This Moment</u> Show Up in 90 Days?

I used to watch a reality TV show called Gold Rush in which several groups of gold miners were filmed going through their process of digging for gold. They used huge construction equipment to scoop up and dump tons of dirt—called paydirt—onto a massive conveyor belt. The conveyor belt would carry the dirt through a filtering process to wash out tiny flecks of gold.

In one show the miners ran their equipment continuously day and night for three days. They used front loaders to scrape paydirt from an area the size of a football field all the way down to bedrock—

about ten feet deep. After three days and tons of dirt, they captured just 27 ounces of gold, which they considered a reasonable success.

On the third day, as the shovel driver was scraping up the final scoops of dirt from the football field-sized claim, he radioed the boss to let him know he was out of paydirt. *"What are we going to run tomorrow?"* he asked in panic. He knew that no matter how good they'd done so far, no paydirt meant no gold. The boss had to locate new areas to dig or there would be no pay*day* for these miners.

Cold doors are your paydirt.

Just like gold, a little bit of result is worth a lot—an ounce of gold was selling for $2,000 when that show was aired. In real estate, one good door is worth many thousands of dollars. You have to sift a lot of paydirt to find it, but it's there.

Your real estate conveyor belt is 90 days long. What you put on that conveyor belt today shows up 90 days from now. If there is a gap in the flow of paydirt, then there will be a corresponding gap in your pay 90 days from now. You can predict the future of your business by looking at how much paydirt you're loading—in the form lead producing activities. The key is to not allow gaps on your conveyor belt.

How Will *This Moment* Show Up in 90 Days?

Technique 3: Recognize Your Compelling Event Threshold

If you've been struggling to put paydirt onto your conveyor belt, then you might have a high Compelling Event (CE) threshold. Simply, this is a condition where you only take action when compelled to by extreme circumstances. In other words, you have to really feel the pain before you'll act.

Here's a simple example to illustrate. Suppose a person has a headlight out on his car. If he has a high CE threshold, he will continue to ignore the headlight as long as possible. He'll drive home every evening in the dark with one headlight out. It might bug him, but what the heck; he'll get by. But then one evening, he gets pulled over and ticketed. The next day he drives to the repair shop and gets the headlight fixed. Getting ticketed was the compelling event that finally made him take action. He could have fixed the headlight proactively at any time and saved himself the embarrassment and expense of the ticket. Instead, *he used the compelling event to give him energy to do the action that needed to be done.*

People do this all the time. They let dirty laundry pile up until there is nothing to wear and they're compelled to do the wash. Listing packages aren't compiled until there's a listing appointment and the agent is compelled to slap something together at the last minute. Rent becomes due and the tenant is compelled to start working hard to find some income—or some trick to buy more time.

Life works so much better when we are proactive about these things. We're more relaxed, more energetic, less frantic and stressed. But some people are wired up to wait. They need compelling events to FORCE them into action. Until then, they'll take the smallest actions possible with the least risk in order to alleviate their discomfort. It's easier to loosen the belt than to go on a diet, right?

Just recognizing this trend in yourself can help you move towards being more proactive. **Ask yourself this pair of questions:**

71

- *Do you tend to wait for compelling events to force you to take action?*
- *Or are you proactive about doing things to move forward—before being compelled by pain?*

Technique 4: Control the Need for Instant Gratification

Some agents don't prospect because they are discouraged when they don't get immediate results. They're hooked into the feeling of instant gratification and can't function simply based on *faith* that their efforts will pay off in the future. They want pay-off now.

I'm reminded of the story of *The Three Little Pigs.* The first two little pigs quickly built their houses out of flimsy stuff so that they could be done and go play. They wanted instant gratification. The third took his time to build a house of brick, knowing he'd be able to play later. We all know what happened when the wolf came calling.

The agent who is willing to delay gratification—having faith that building a strong foundation brick by brick will pay off in the end— is the agent who will succeed.

Real estate agents are notorious for being seduced by expensive offers of instant gratification that make outrageous claims: "Get listings in 24 hours without lifting a finger or spending a dime with our new, patented listing program!" These agents build houses of straw, so they can run out and play. They take long lunches, go shopping, do non-effective networking that looks like work, etc. People who chronically put self-gratification ahead of self-discipline will struggle in this business.

Catch-22

These agents are in a self-imposed Catch-22, refusing to work hard until they see the payoff—but unlikely to see a payoff until they work hard at it. (Catch-22 is a paradoxical situation from which an individual cannot escape because of contradictory rules.)

To overcome this problem, agents must commit to a period of time during which they must have faith without expectation of stunning results. Ideally, when starting a program of door knocking, agents will have enough money or source of income to allow them 90 days of low productivity as they ramp up. This gives them the luxury of time to see a payoff.

Ask yourself these questions:

- *When the wolf is at your door, will you look back and wish you'd taken more time to build a strong foundation when you had the time?*
- *Are you taking longer lunches and coffee breaks than you really need? Are you getting into work late? Are you quitting early?*
- **How many hours are you REALLY working each week?**
- *Do you believe door knocking can work?*
- *Do you believe it 100%?*
- *If not, are you at least willing to give it 100% effort for 90 days? If not 90, can you give it at least 30 days?*

Technique 5: Disappear the Fear

Disappear the Fear is a technique borrowed from hypnotherapy. The technique is often used to help people overcome phobias. (As in *"You're afraid of falling...but you're not really falling. So the fear is a* feeling, *not a real event that is happening."*) Nothing bad happens in door knocking, beyond someone saying *no* to you. But we feel afraid of it. Hearing *no* raises all sorts of scary feelings that started in our childhoods. By the time we're adults, we've internalized these fears, even though they make no objective sense.

If you're afraid of prospecting, recognize that it's just a *feeling.* There are no physical, social, or spiritual consequences to door knocking except what's between your ears.

Eleanor Roosevelt famously said, *"No one can make you feel inferior without your consent."* Or as W.C. Fields put it: *"It ain't what they call you, it's what you answer to."*

If prospecting is critical to the welfare of your family and to the fulfillment of your dreams, then you can't let someone else control your feelings. Try this techniques to get past the fear:

Where Is the Fear in Your Body?

Fear is an automatic response designed to protect us from negative situations. The fear makes us pay attention so we can avoid something bad. But fear has a time limit. We can't avoid the fear, but we can wait it out. This technique makes use of that time limit on fear.

- When you feel afraid of prospecting, take a moment to sit quietly without distractions. Close your eyes so you can focus inwardly.

- Next, feel the fear in your body. Fear for many people can be pinpointed to a physical location, as in *"My stomach is in knots,"* or *"I can't catch my breath,"* or *"I have a lump in my throat,"* or *"I have butterflies in my stomach,"* or *"My shoulders are so tight they feel like they're going to break."*

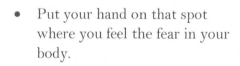

- Put your hand on that spot where you feel the fear in your body.

- Focus your full attention on that spot under your hand. Allow your thoughts to come and go, but bring your attention back to the physical focal point under your hand. Don't make up stories about the fear. Just be with the *feeling* of the fear under your hand. Try to notice the fear without thinking about what it means. Notice the fear as a feeling under your hand.

- After a minute, narrow the focus under your hand to a pinpoint. Put all of the intensity of the fear into that pinpoint. Imagine that feeling of fear as a tiny, intense point of light under your hand. Make the point of light smaller and smaller to a pinprick of intensity.

- Stay with that focus. At some point you will notice that the fear seems to have passed or disappeared and you don't feel it anymore. It can take a few minutes — or even longer, but it will disappear completely by itself.

- Repeat as necessary if the fear returns.

Technique 6: Modelling

In the study of Neurolinguistic Programming (NLP), researchers have shown that the brain records communication in specific patterns, inclusive of grammar, tone, volume, facial motions, and eye movements. Humans use these communication patterns to communicate internally with ourselves as much as externally. Our communication patterns are so consistent that they can be copied—modelled—by others to achieve the exact same results as the original behaviors. So if a hypnotist is able to convince someone to stop smoking, then someone else who models the exact same intonations, facial gestures, language, etc. as the hypnotist would be able to stop someone else from smoking, even if they didn't know a thing about hypnosis.

The encoding of performance in our movements and language can be useful. For instance, the direction of eye movement has been shown to indicate thought processes, such as lying, remembering, and imagining. Policemen can detect if a person is lying by the direction their eyes move when they're talking, because they can tell if the person is imagining their answer or remembering it.

By knowing how humans encode certain behaviors and thoughts linguistically, NLP therapists can sometimes help a person change an unwanted behavior (such as smoking) in an instant by addressing the underlying programming. Unscrupulous people (including many salespeople) can use these patterns to influence people's decisions without their awareness.

Perhaps the best known practitioner of NLP is Tony Robbins, of *The Giant Within* fame. Tony has a gift for motivation, which is in large part due to his expert ability to use NLP to help his audience access and unlock different parts of their psyche.

As real estate agents, NLP can be enormously useful in overcoming fears. When we model an expert performer who seems fearless to us, we can get similar results—both internally and externally. In other words, we feel less fear and seem less fearful to others when we model the patterns these experts use.

Fortunately, this is not difficult to do. We already unconsciously do it whenever we listen to good trainers and speakers, like Tony Robbins, Mike Ferry, Joe Stumpf, Brian Buffini, etc.

That's one of the reasons we like going to workshops and speaking engagements. We feel good because we internalize those expert behaviors, tone of voice, and attitude—in addition to their messages. Our motions and words and feelings for a time afterwards will mirror theirs and we feel great about ourselves—our self-doubts minimized.

You can use this skill consciously any time you want by listening to recordings and watching videos of various experts. This is, in my opinion, the key reason to listen to motivational speakers in your car on the way to appointments or to go door knocking. For a time after listening, you will retain and exude some of their expertise, enthusiasm, and confidence.

Attitude in, attitude out!

Technique 7: Take Five

Perhaps the simplest technique for getting past prospecting reluctance is to commit to a short burst of time or activity—five minutes, five rounds, five actions, five of something. For example, if you don't want to do the dishes, perhaps you can commit to doing just five dishes instead of the whole sink full. Or if you don't like folding the laundry, you can agree with yourself to fold just five items. When finished with that five, chances are you will keep going. If not, commit to another five. Then another.

If you resist door knocking, perhaps you can commit to just five doors or five minutes or five contacts. Once you complete those five, perhaps you will want to do another five. Perhaps you can decide to do five rounds of five.

When I'm feeling tired, I'll door knock until I talk to five people, even if I must knock on twenty doors to do it. By the time I've spoken to the first five people, I feel pretty good about talking to another five people. Before I know it, I've spoken to ten, then twenty people.

Of course, sometimes I talk to five people and quit. But at least I spoke to five!

Chapter 5:
Door Knocking Scripts

Basically, there are three different layers of scripting to learn:

- **Openers**—what you say when they open the door.
- **Follow-on Questions**—what you say after they say *yes* or *maybe*.
- **Getting Appointments and Next Steps**—how you secure an appointment or permission to stay in contact.

First, let's address two factors that make a huge difference in how you are received:

- **Attitude at the Door**
- **How to Crack the Ice of a Cold Door**

Attitude at the Door

Your attitude clings to you like a suit of clothes. People can see it and feel it. They respond to it both consciously and subconsciously. If you wear a warm smile and a positive "I'm supposed to be here" attitude, you'll get the same back from them. If you have a nervous attitude or look harassed, you'll get doors shut in your face. If you feel uncertain, they will feel uncertain about you.

Do you know someone who exudes confidence? There's something about the way they stand, hold their mouth, even the glint in their eye. Their physiology mirrors their internal attitude.

Fortunately, the reverse is also true—physiology can *affect* your attitude, not just mirror it. A person can consciously stand a certain way, hold their mouth a certain way, speak with a certain voice, and their attitude will begin to shift towards believing it.

Actors use this knowledge to be convincing in a role from the inside out. You can use the same skill to improve your results. When your attitude is amazing, you'll get listings.

If you want people to deal positively with you, then act like a hero. Be there to make their upcoming move the best move of their life! The more *certain* you appear, the more confident they will feel about you.

Fake It 'til You Make It

If you don't feel confident and certain, if you're nervous or don't believe in what you're doing yet, what can you do? You can fake it 'til you make it.

How do you do that? You take a deep breath, smile broadly, and speak firmly without apology. You can think to yourself "big sloppy grin." It knocks the seriousness right out of you. You can imagine yourself as an actor/actress on stage performing the part of a high-volume listing agent—the prospect doesn't know you're not a high-volume listing agent unless you show them otherwise with your attitude. You can also stop worrying about getting it right and just be willing to look foolish, make mistakes, and learn as you go. People respond very well to vulnerability in someone with a confident demeanor.

Openers

Door knocking is all about the first moments—your energy and your words. Speak at a measured pace with certainty and enthusiasm. You want them to hear and process what you're saying. Don't speak quickly or mumble.

Always start by saying some form of:

"Hi, my name is _____ and I'm a real estate agent with _____."

If you have a long or obscure company name that says nothing about real estate (for instance, my previous company was called Rex Downing and Associates), you may simply want to say that you're a real estate agent, without mentioning a company name.

Depending on your situation, you can follow your introduction with any of these different openers:

1. Generic Openers
2. Just Listed Openers
3. I Have a Buyer Openers
4. Just Sold Openers
5. Open House Invitation Openers
6. Vacant House Openers
7. Geographic Farm Openers

None of the following phrases are set in stone. You can alter the wording as you go, depending on what flows best from you. Pick one to begin with and practice it. Then when you're door knocking for real, you'll get a feeling for what works best for you.

Generic Openers

- *"I'm wondering if you folks are planning a move in the next year or so?"*

- *"I was just wondering if you've been thinking about selling your home in the near future?"*

- *"I'm wondering if you know anyone in the neighborhood who might be thinking about moving or have a reason to sell?"*

Remember, practice and find the best words for yourself. I have found the word *wondering* to be a softener that works for me.

Just Listed Openers

- *"We just listed a house nearby, and I'm wondering who you know who wants to buy a home?"*

"I Have a Buyer" Openers

- *"I have a buyer looking for a home in this neighborhood, and they haven't found the right home yet, so I was wondering if you are planning on moving in the near future and might want to talk about selling your home?"*

I realize this is long, but it is effective. The average home owner is surprised to see an agent at their door. If you have a reason for being there, it takes the surprise and suspicion away. Be ready to add more depth to the story about your home buyers.

I only use this approach when it's absolutely true, though I know agents who use this all the time, true or not, then justify it by saying that once they get the listing, they will have a buyer for it.

By the way, when you offer choices, people tend to focus only on the second part of the choice. So if you say *"I was wondering if you **or someone you know** is planning on moving in the near future?"* the prospect will only focus on *someone you know.*

Just Sold Openers

- *"I just sold the house down the street at _____, and I'm wondering if you folks have been thinking about selling your home, too?"*

- *"You know, we just sold a house nearby and now have a list of buyers who want to live in the area. Do you know anyone else who might be thinking about selling? ... Would you be thinking about moving yourselves in the near future?"*

Open House Invitation Openers

- *"I've just listed a new home over on _____ and I'd like to invite you to an open house this _____. Do you know anyone who's looking for a house and might be interested in this neighborhood?"*

Sometimes I like to have a little fun and will say something like:

- *"Hi, it's _____ with _____. I've just sold (or listed) a new home over on _____. Would you like to guess what it sold for (or selling for)?"*

Vacant House Openers

- *"I'm following up on the property next door/across the street/down the road that's vacant and wondering if you know anything about it/how to get in touch with the owners?"*

Sometimes just showing up and asking homeowners about their plans will result in business. For example see the following story.

***

As Easy As It Gets
by Katie Burmeister, Keller Williams, St. Louis MO

I went door knocking for the first time a couple months ago. I went in the area/neighborhood in which I want to farm. I recently had a home sold in the neighborhood. I created a flyer with some info about the area (stats on the market, recently sold homes, info about the community such as a 5K run). My script is "Hello, I'm the Realtor who just sold the home down the street. Here is some info about your neighborhood. By the way do you know anyone looking to buy or sell?"

Well, I got 2 listing appointments and 1 buyer out of it for about 3 hours of work. Not ONE person was rude or standoffish. Several people engaged in conversation with me in regards to real estate even though they weren't interested in buying or selling.

Since then I continue to door knock and I get at least one hot lead out of it every time I go out. The cost of door knocking is almost free, it's a great way to get your name out there and it's great exercise.

I'm sure this approach won't work everywhere but it has worked for me so far. And in all honesty, once you get the hang of it and once your confidence builds up it's about as easy as it gets.

***

Geographic Farm Openers

If you're doing regular door knocking in a farm, you might vary your openers, especially if homeowners recognize you. Always introduce yourself first, then follow-on with questions like these:

- *"Hi, it's _____ again, agent with _____…*

- *"Prices are going up in the area and I thought you might like to see what's been selling."*

- *"I'm holding an open house at _____ and wonder if you'd like to stop by this Sunday for some cookies?"*

- *"Now that prices have risen so sharply in the area, I'm wondering if you've begun to think about selling?"*

- *"I thought I'd stop by and see if you know anyone who'd be interested in buying a great home in the area that hasn't been listed yet."*

- *"One of your neighbors is the owner of Tasty Pastries and he's offering a free croissant to all area residents I meet today. Would you like one?" (Great way to build strategic alliances.)*

How to Crack the Ice of a Cold Door

Sometimes people are reluctant to give information too soon, but if you can get them talking for a few minutes, they suddenly tell you that the house across the street is vacant and you should call the owner, or their son is thinking about buying. If you can engage in a longer conversation, you can often get more information.

Here's one easy way to extend the conversation. Most people are proud of their homes. It takes very little energy to tap into that pride at the door. If you feel like they're being friendly to your opener, add a simple comment, like *"I love the way you designed your garden." "Your lawn looks like a putting green." "That's a beautiful entryway." "Your roses are spectacular." "I love the color of your house."* You can unlock a flood of friendly good-will that will lead to all sorts of information about the neighborhood and who's going to be moving next. Just pick something that obviously matters to them.

When I feel the person at the door has the right energy, I might say something ironic, like *"Do you ever plan to put wheels on that car or is it more like a piece of sculpture?"* That's my personality, so it works.

Example: Using an Ice Breaker to Extend the Conversation

People often ask if I follow a script or just converse spontaneously. I always follow a script...until a certain point. Then I rely on conversation patterns. For example:

"Hi, my name is Linda with Windermere Real Estate. I was just wondering if you've been thinking about selling your home in the near future?" [No.] *"OK, thanks. By the way, you have the nicest roses I've ever seen."* [Oh, thank you. My husband spends hours on them.] *"Really? What does a person do for hours on their roses?"* [Laughter. He...blah, blah, blah.] *"You seem to have lived in the area a long time. Do you know a lot of your neighbors?"* [Oh, yes. We've lived here for 20 years. The Jones' across the street have been here nearly as long, and the ...

etc.] *"I'm sorry to hear that Mr. Smith has passed away. Do you have any idea what they plan to do with the house now?"*

Notice that I always use a statement-question pattern. I make a statement, then ask a question. I make another statement reflecting their answer, then ask another question. I repeat this pattern, drawing them in the direction I want the conversation to go.

The information you gather during these longer conversations can be used as you continue door knocking. By the end of your second hour, you'll sound like you've represented that neighborhood for years. You'll be able to talk about the Jones' new baby, the Smith's recent death, the Krueger's hummingbirds, the ugly addition the Crankmeyers just put on, etc. You'll sound less and less like a stranger the more conversations you have.

After finishing longer conversations, try to get the owner's name, address, phone number, and email address. At the office later, put a hand-written thank-you note in the mail, commenting again on the hummingbirds or roses. If you got an email address, put them into your fully automated follow up system.

Follow-On Questions

After knocking, asking your opening, and then hearing *yes,* you'll want to be prepared with a series of follow-on questions. The *yeses* will take you by surprise, so be ready. Here are suggestions.

Mike Ferry Questions

Devotees of Mike Ferry are familiar with the following series of questions (or some variations):

1. *"When do you plan on moving?"*
2. *"How long have you lived at this address?"*
3. *"Where did you move from?"*
4. *"If you were to move, where would you go next?"*
5. *"And when would that be?"*
6. *"It takes about _____ months to sell a house in the current market. Did you know that?"*
7. *"Did you want to start selling in _____, or did you want to be moved already by that time?"*
8. *"Then the next thing we should do is…"*

This is a great series of questions, and valuable to memorize. (By the way, the Mike Ferry organization provides solid real estate coaching, so check them out at **www.mikeferry.com**.)

At the same time, don't expect to use all these questions or use them in this order. For instance, you may get a *yes* that sounds something like this:

> ▪ *"Yes, we have been thinking about selling. My husband was just offered a job in Phoenix and we might have to move by January. We've only been here a year, so I'm not sure how much our house is worth and if we can even afford to sell it."*

In that case, it would feel very awkward to start asking this series of questions. An alternative—or really an addition—is to practice a natural, openhanded selling pattern that allows the conversation to be more flexible. See below.

Openhanded Selling

Openhanded Selling relies on using clean questions to direct a conversation without pressure. Start by using what the prospect's own comments to dictate your next responses. Let's use the example just given:

- *"Yes, we have been thinking about selling. My husband was just offered a job in Phoenix and we might have to move by January. We've only been here a year, so I'm not sure how much our house is worth and if we can even afford to sell it."*

1. First, **reflect** their feeling or comments without offering solutions. Then attach a **question** about what they've done to deal with the situation. Remember, it's reflect/question:

   - *"You sound stressed by all the uncertainty. What have you done already to prepare, just in case the promotion does come through?"*

2. Continue to probe for their ideas using the same **reflect/question** format. Use *what happened* to encourage them to expand:

   - *"So you've just started to investigate selling. Have you already checked into what your home is worth? ... **What happened?** ... I see. You were disappointed in the prices you saw. Have you already spoken to a real estate agent to get a specific price on your home? ... **What happened?** The agent didn't offer you any hope. What did you think as a result of that conversation? ..."*

3. Transition to an openhanded close. This is a close that gives them the opportunity to say no. This is unlike traditional sales. But if you've created rapport and they really do see the value in talking to you, they'll say yes.

- *"You know, I have some ideas about price. Would you like to hear them?"*

4. Set the appointment while addressing any suspected objections. Don't wait for them to voice those objections. In this example, price is an objection, as well as uncertainty about the timing of the sale. You could say:

   - *"So price is a function of what buyers are willing to pay for what they see. I think there are few things you could do to raise the value of your home by changing what buyers are seeing.*

   - *Also, it may not matter what you want from your house. If you need to move, you have to sell...but at least you want as much as you can get, right?*

   - *Also, it takes about two weeks to get an offer in this market, and 30 days after that to close. That means getting your home on the market about six weeks before you have to move...so that would be by next Thursday. That's probably sooner than you thought. So we should probably talk about options available to you if you have to sell quickly when the promotion happens.*

   - *I can meet you this Thursday at 6 pm. Will that give your husband time to get home from work?"*

Getting Appointments and Next Step Commitments

Great agents ask for business reflexively. Their closing is the logical outcome of the conversation and prospects are ready — even eager to be asked. By contrast, when unpracticed agents ask for business, they can sound desperate or uncertain, and that feeling telegraphs itself to the prospective client.

For this reason, I believe that a key skill for real estate agents to practice is *asking for appointments.*

Let's look at how real estate agents can shoot themselves in the foot by asking in an unpracticed, unskilled manner. Below are two agent responses to a prospect. One is a skilled response and the other is an unskilled response:

- **Prospect:** *"Well, we're probably going to start talking about selling after Christmas."*

- **Less skilled response:** *"May I stay in touch with you?"*

- **More skilled response:** *"Then it sounds like we should get together in early January to go over your selling plans. How's the fourth sound to you?"*

There are many ways to ask for an appointment. Even if you're taken by surprise and only have the presence of mind to blurt out *"Well, could I try out for the job?"* you're doing more than most agents.

The real problem is not how you ask; the real problem is *not* asking at all. The simple fact of not asking for appointments sabotages more real estate careers than any other single thing other than prospecting reluctance.

How many times have you failed to ask for a phone number at an open house, or failed to ask buyers to meet at your office before showing homes, or failed to ask a friend if they'd connect you with their relative who's selling, or other similar situations?

How often have you resisted prospecting or marketing activities because you were afraid of asking? How often have you kicked yourself after learning your hot lead went with someone else?

Asking increases the odds of *getting. Not asking* eliminates the odds of getting altogether. The choice is clear.

How to Nail-Down the <u>Appointment</u>

Rather than using the word "closing," which seems fraught with angst, I prefer to talk about securing or nailing down the appointment.

When you knock on someone's door and start talking to them about real estate, their thoughts and plans might be all over the place. By nailing down the appointment, you're offering them a secure starting point. You're helping them bring focus to their plans.

Practice nail-down questions:

- *"How's ___ sound?" This is really a yes/no question that they can't answer with a simple yes or no. Examples: "How's Thursday sound to you?" "How's the ninth of March sound to you?"*

- *"Would you be interested in ___ on ___?" Examples: "Would you be interested in <u>seeing that house</u> on <u>Wednesday</u>?" "Would you be interested in <u>getting that list</u> by <u>Friday</u>?" "Would you be interested in <u>discussing your plans</u> in <u>two weeks on Sunday after church</u>?"*

- *"I have some time on ___, or would you prefer ___?" This is a classic nail-down question, but it still works, especially when worded in this way. Example: "I have some time on Wednesday evening, or would you prefer Thursday?"*

Nail-Down a <u>Next Step</u> (If No Appointment)

If they're moving within six months, nail the appointment. But if they're moving after six months, you may want to settle for nailing down an intermediate step. You can always nail the appointment another time, provided you've followed up consistently.

A good next step is to gain their consent to stay in touch. I like to offer something that puts them on my mailing list. For example:

> ■ *"I've got a <u>great newsletter that helps home sellers get more money out of their homes when they sell</u>. Would you like me to put you on my mailing list so that when I contact you again, you'll know that I know what I'm talking about?"*

I'm offering something of value **and** telling them why it's valuable. It might be a newsletter, or something else. Then I'm reminding them that I'll be back in touch and planting a seed in their minds.

I sometimes will carry copies of my newsletter and if our rapport is very good, I will walk them quickly through the newsletter, pointing out features and benefits. In doing that, I further anchor in the value. They'll look forward to getting it each month in the mail, and they'll also remember me with greater clarity.

Handling Objections to Setting Appointments

Many people will wonder why the heck you want to set a appointment for three months from now. Some people will have objections. When you know the objections in advance, you can practice your responses:

Objection 1

> ■ **Prospect:** *"No thanks. We're planning on selling ourselves."*

> ■ **You:** *"I understand you wanting to save the money. I still have something to offer you where you get all your money and more. See, I know everything a person with 20 years experience can know about selling a house, staying out of legal hot water, and winning at negotiations. I'd like to let you pick my brain. Find out everything you can about selling yourself. That way, if you do change your mind or if something doesn't work out, you'll*

know that I know what I'm talking about and perhaps under those circumstances you'll want to reach out to me. I'll give you 30 minutes of my time and you can ask me all the questions you want. Fair enough?"

Objection 2

- **Prospect:** *"We're not sure which agent we'll be using. We'll let you know."*

- **You:** *"I think you'll find I'm an aggressive negotiator, and I know what it takes to market a house, qualify buyers, field other agents, hold open houses, negotiate deals, manage the inspections, negotiate repairs, protect you legally, and get the most money possible for you. [Add something personally important to them if you can.] Have I piqued your interest enough to earn an interview in early March for the job of selling your home?"*

Objection 3

- **Prospect:** *"We're not sure when we'll be moving, but it'll probably be next year some time."*

- **You:** *"It is hard to plan that far ahead, isn't it? Since you don't know what's going to happen for sure yet, I'd like to give you a copy of my **12-Month Home Selling Improvement Plan**. This will help you do all the right things a little at a time on your house over the next year.*

  People who work through this list make between $5,000 and $20,000 more when they sell than people who wait until the last minute. Would you find that to be valuable? [Yes.] What's the best way for me to get this home selling improvement plan to you? I can drop it by in hard copy or email it. [Email.] What email address?

The Art behind Handling Objections

Objection-handling requires nothing more than preparation and practice. Along with jotting down all of the typical objections you get and focusing on the exact words you would use to handle each, also focus on the intention behind your words. In particular, 1) acknowledge their concerns, 2) offer an expert solution, and 3) ask a lot of questions, including tie-down questions. Tie-down questions are those that get them to make small commitments...*Email or phone? Valuable or not?* etc.

A great telemarketer once told me that the more questions you can get someone to answer, the more likely you are to make the sale. I tried it out, doing telemarketing for her online listing service for just one day, and she was absolutely right. The more questions I asked—even if they were inane, light-weight, and irrelevant—the more likely I was to make a sale.

Chapter 6:
Fanatical Follow-Up

Don't Drop the Ball

If there's one absolute in selling, it's this: Most sales occur in the follow up, not in the initial contact.

Research has shown time and time again that top salespeople attribute their success, not to any glib sales techniques, but to following up consistently. Consider a study by the National Association of Sales Professionals which found that 80% of all non-retail sales are made between the 5th and 12th follow up contact.

Yet this and other studies show that most salespeople give up after just 3 or 4 contacts, while as many as 48% of salespeople never follow up at all after the initial contact!

Don't drop the ball. Get your message in front of your leads repeatedly from the moment of your initial introduction until they do business with you, refer someone to you, or tell you to stop contacting them!

This may seem drastic, but who's going to be contacting them if you're not? Someone else will, if you don't. And when the prospect decides to hire *that* person to buy or sell their house, it won't be because your service didn't meet their needs. It will be because you weren't top-of-mind for them. Don't expect your leads to remember you. Make certain they by using a combination of passive and active follow up communication.

Fill Your Pipeline

I once heard a remarkable door knocking agent say that his goal with door knocking was to fill his pipeline of future business so deep and wide that he'd never have to worry about money again. If that were you, imagine how business would flow peacefully to you and all the problems related to your finances would vanish.

A pipeline—for those of you unfamiliar with the term—is a plumbing metaphor used in sales. If your pipeline is full, you can turn the tap and get a flow of business going. If your pipeline is empty, you'll get a trickle, if anything. Your pipeline should be full of warm leads that have come from door knocking, referral sources, other prospecting sources, and past clients. A warm lead is someone who's said they have plans to move, usually within the next year or two.

Be careful not to add *fake leads* to your pipeline. (Review **Fake Leads**.)

Keep in mind as you read this section that there are at least two different types of people that you will want to follow up with. The two main types are your SOI list and your Leads list. You can, of course, segment your lists in many different ways. For instance, your SOI list could be segmented by A-level, B-level, and so on. Your Leads list can be segmented based on hot and warm, buyer and seller, etc.

Let's focus in this chapter just on Lead follow up.

Your Lead Follow-Up Plan

A lead follow up plan should contain both active and passive follow up. Active follow up means physically contacting them. Passive follow up means creating and using the mail and internet to automatically deliver content to them—a set and forget system.

The Active Component

The active component of your follow up plan consists of a simple series of touch-points:

1. Send a thank you note the same day you meet them.
2. Call a day or two after sending the note to see if they got it and to remind them of what you talked about at the door. *"When we talked, you said you were moving in a year and a half when you retire. Is that about right?"*
3. Add their name to a passive drip campaign. Note: Some agents will spend time creating a specialized drip campaign just for each particular type of lead (buyer warm; buyer hot; seller warm; seller hot). You can do that. However, if you don't have the time or knowledge to create separate campaigns, simply using the same generic campaign for everyone is better than nothing!
4. Depending on their moving plans, call back every two to three days, weeks, or months. Once people start thinking about moving, they tend to speed up their plans. You don't want to call a month before the date of their planned move only to find out they just closed. **Position yourself as the obvious expert through regular call-backs and consistent mailings.**

The Passive Component

There are two types of passive follow-up system you should have in your business. There's the drip campaigns you use to follow up with leads and the monthly or quarterly mailings you send to your entire SOI list.

Put your Leads on your SOI mailing plan—but don't put your SOI onto your drip campaigns for Leads. There will be plenty of people on your SOI list who are not leads and never will be leads—but are potential sources of referrals. You'll be sending them a monthly or quarterly newsletter, as well as occasional extras, like a calendar, proof of success story, etc. Your Leads list should also get these mailings.

In addition, your Leads list will get a specialized drip campaign. Set this up using an email service or program, like MailChimp, Aweber, Top Producer, etc.

The drip campaign should consist of very short (150 words) tips, stories, and offers. These should go out at least weekly. They should be very heavy on value. Give away a secret. Give away a coupon. Give away a link. Give away a report or ebook. Following are details about different kinds of follow up offers you can provide.

Follow-Up Offers

Service Provider Discounts

One of my favorite follow up strategies is to partner with strategic alliance partners who can provide a service or gift to your database. For instance, my carpet cleaner offers 50% off coupon just to my clients and leads. He loses money on the deal, but gains new clients, and I refer him constantly to other Realtors.

In this arrangement, the service provider benefits from increased business, your leads and clients benefit from the service, and you get to be the hero who sent the offer to them.

Make sure the offer from the service provider is significant. Think of the kinds of offers you see on Groupon and be sure the offer will make someone sit up and take notice. Otherwise they'll simply start to treat your mail as junk mail. Send these offers as postcards or stand-alone emails.

Where there is a need, it seems that someone can create a business to satisfy that need, and The Referral Squirrel is a prime example. Check out **www.thereferralsquirrel.com** to see what they do. They set up service provider discounts, print the postcards, and even mail them for you! The only suggestion I have for you to improve results is to create a referral relationship with the service provider that is giving the gift. Let them know that you would go above and beyond for them if they would reciprocate by sending a similar postcard to their customers recommending YOU.

This postcard comes from a great referral service at www.thereferralsquirrel.com

Newsletters

A newsletter is a traditional marketing tool used for decades by companies to slip their sales messages "under the radar" by mixing their marketing in with other kinds of information.

Unlike direct mail advertising, newsletters tend to be viewed as informative and interesting.

Since people are less resistant to reading of this kind, most people read newsletters with their guards down, allowing your messages in. Your readers won't always realize that they're reading something that may cause them to be more loyal and committed to you.

Fast Newsletters

Fast, original real estate newsletters just $9/month!

Fast Newsletters provides a flexible real estate newsletter, pre-written from scratch by real estate marketing experts. They put thought into every newsletter... asking themselves, "What will clients find interesting? What will they want to know? What will make them remember this agent? What will make them call this agent?"

The newsletters come in MS Word, so you can personalize your newsletter in just minutes by changing the easy placeholders (red text). You can also customize any aspect of the newsletter. Nothing is locked. Drop by for more information: www.FastNewsletters.com.

Content of Newsletters

The key is connecting with your readers in a way that is meaningful to them. You are only *slightly* meaningful to them. The real estate industry is only *slightly* meaningful to them unless they're planning to move soon. So most newsletter experts agree that the real secret to successful newsletters is the "other stuff" that's not about you or your business.

It's the light-hearted and short stories, funny anecdotes, quizzes, and interesting facts that people take to the reading room (bathroom) with them. They look forward to that newsletter.

When writing your own newsletter, create little stories that are fun to read. Slip in a little real estate information in the form of around-the-house articles like, "Staging Secrets You Can Do on Your Own." Add under-the-radar reminders that you're in real estate. For instance, at the end of a staging article, you can add that you have a staging service available to help them sell faster.

Newsletters can be as simple as a two-sided sheet of paper with a few interesting tid-bits, like a personal note, a real estate message, and perhaps something funny or timely for the season. Other forms of newsletters include a classified ads sheet, a list of jokes (and almost nothing else!), a list great real estate deals currently on the market, a blog that does double-duty as a newsletter, and a DIY projects newsletter. Whatever you choose to do, give it a catchy name, be consistent in what you send, and be consistent in sending it.

Hard Copy or Emailed Newsletters?

This is an enduring argument. I like using hard copy for my core SOI list and my Hot Leads. I expect a lot from them, so I want them to feel my presence physically. I also like to hand-deliver my newsletters to my farm, especially on a warm Saturday when a lot of people are out front of their houses.

Then I have bunch of other contacts that I've picked up along the way at networking events and other connections. They get my newsletter emailed to them automatically.

Which works better?

Some agents don't like the added expense of printing and mailing, so they prefer emailing. Does it work as well as hard-copy?

Experiments show...that it depends. Among the people who already know, like, and trust you, physical mail is perceived as "special," rather than being considered junk mail. However, if you already have an e-relationship with people through Facebook or another electronic source, then an emailed newsletter performs just as well as a physical one.

When deciding if you want to send a hard copy or email newsletter, consider how you know people and if they're more tuned into electronic communications with you or not.

One agent I know in Carlsbad is a leader in his local cycling club. He sends his e-newsletter to all 800 members of the cycling club, as well as his leads and past clients. They are used to communicating about their cycling events through email, so his e-newsletter fits right in. By weaving important cycling news into his real estate content, he gives people a reason to open the email. In addition, they see him at cycling events regularly, further reinforcing the desire to open his newsletter to keep in touch with him. He gets nearly 100% of his business from fellow cyclists and their referrals.

On the other hand, if you are not typically connected to your group by email, or if your group is unlikely to have similar casual interests, you may have more difficulty getting them to open your email regularly. I get an email every month from my financial planner. I really enjoy chatting with her the occasional times when we get together. But her emailed newsletters are boring.

When I'm looking at my email, I'm not looking for another thing to read online. I'm looking for quick communications that are useful or valuable to me in the moment. Who knows what valuable information I'm missing by ignoring her newsletters? More importantly for her, who knows how often I might think of someone to send her way if she was more top-of-mind?

Social Media Follow Up

Basically, the rule of thumb for using social media to follow up is this: If your SOI list is largely on social media, you can use it to follow up. If not, don't make it a core part of your follow up strategy—unless you have an assistant who can post for you. Do not use social media alone to follow up with *Leads*.

Tchatchka—Bumpy Mailings

Brian Buffini created a whole business out of providing a subscription to real estate agents where they would get a monthly item of value to pass on to people on their SOI list. These included note cards for hand-written notes, as well as small items like a pin or credit card letter opener.

Once placed into an envelope, these make the envelope bumpy—so they are often called "bumpy mailings." Everyone loves a gift. I've met raving fans who wax poetic about their real estate agents simply because the agent sends them a little pin each month. It's not about the real estate!

Proof of Success Stories

Each month, tell a story about one specific real estate problem you solved for one specific client. This will serve as both illustration and testimonial. Then send this as a postcard monthly, as an email, or as part of your newsletter. If possible, use a picture of the person or people you helped. People love real stories, and these are a great way to connect. You can also send these via social media. They do not have to be written by the client as testimonials. You can write them about the client's experience from your perspective, with their permission. You can also make them up.

What's Your Call to Action?

If you plan to mail postcards, be sure to include a strong call to action. A weak call to action sounds like this: *"Call me for all your real estate needs."*

A strong call to action includes an offer, like these:

- *"Call me to schedule a free 30 minute staging consultation."*

- *"Wondering how much your house has risen in value this year? Text me your address and I'll text back an estimate."*

Your Business Exit Strategy

A great warm lead pipeline is a valuable commodity. By following up consistently, you can track your results. Over a few years, you'll know your numbers. You'll know how many of your warm leads actually perform. You'll know the best ways to communicate with them. You'll have, possibly, well over a hundred warm leads in your pipeline that will do something in the next two years, not to mention refer others to you.

Suppose you want to spend the next couple of years on vacation in Europe or tootling around in your RV? Wouldn't it be nice to hand all that business to someone else and have them run it for the next two to five years, giving you a fat 30% referral fee for each closing?

Only a fanatical follow-up system will give you that level of freedom.

Summary:
Set Up Your Door Knocking Program

To create a high-production door-knocking program in your real estate business, take the following steps:

1. Decide what kind of door knocking you'll be doing: continuous, farm, or purpose-driven. Write out a schedule of when and where you'll knock. Create a firm commitment to your schedule. Consider using an accountability coach who will hold your feet to the fire. (See **Chapter 2: Door Knocking Strategies**.)

2. Review the FAQ's from Chapter 1. (See **Chapter 1: Realities of Door Knocking/FAQs**.) But don't get hung up on specifics. The very best way to train yourself is to go do it!

3. If you haven't already done so, write a business plan. It will save you countless hours of spinning your wheels.

4. Write out two door knocking opener(s) you'll use for your chosen approach. Practice them until they flow smoothly off the tongue. (See **Chapter 5, subsection: Openers**.)

    *** Go practice now....then continue preparing.***

5. Write out your lead follow-on questions. Get someone to practice with you, until you can easily address some of the typical kinds of responses you'll get to your openings. (See **Chapter 5, subsection: Follow-On Questions**.)

6. Write out your appointment and next step questions. Practice asking for the appointment. (See **Chapter 5, subsection: Asking for an Appointment**.)

7. Prepare your follow up plan. Have your first newsletter ready to go for the next month. Have a database system set up so you can put names into it from the start. (See **Chapter 6: Fanatical Follow Up**.)

8. Put together your door knocking wardrobe and paraphernalia. You shouldn't have to think about this every morning. Treat it like a uniform. The fewer steps between you and getting out the door, the easier it will be to door knock. (See **Chapter 1, FAQ: What to Wear.**)

9. Prepare and practice your listing presentation. The more you are READY to LIST, the more likely you'll telegraph that you are a competent listing agent. Remember that your energy does most of the "selling" for you.

Happy hunting!

Linda Schneider

About the Author

Linda Schneider is a real estate agent, trainer, coach, and author. Like many real estate agents, she did not start her career as a Realtor. Her background as a linguist and adult language educator with USAID led her into corporate training when she was invited to develop training programs for the Franklin Covey Company.

While with Franklin Covey, Ms. Schneider developed a real estate training program for a major brokerage. Real estate captivated her. She took her license and began selling. Then, in 2000 she was tapped to be a nationwide trainer with By Referral Only.

To date, she has written and developed more than a thousand real estate and sales training products and led coaching programs for brokerages and corporations in all major English speaking countries. She currently divides her time between writing, speaking, raising a family, and *still* selling real estate.

If you would like to contact Linda Schneider about speaking at your event, or for any other reason, you can email her at: **contact@agentsonfire.com.**

Bonus Chapter:
Openhanded Selling

Following is an introduction to a consultative selling approach called Openhanded Selling.

A Different Relationship to Selling

You may have heard the term *consultative selling* before. You might have also heard the terms *soft selling, sales counseling, solution coaching, sales consultant,* or *real estate consultant.* What all these terms have in common is the philosophical idea of *helping* clients rather than simply forcing a solution on them. The hope is that by helping clients, the clients will discover that they need the solution you're offering.

The *idea* of soft or consultative selling is appealing to real estate agents. The words sound giving and "heart-centered" and pleasant. By contrast, traditional or *hard* selling sounds painful. Frankly, most agents would rather eat rotten fruit than use objection-handling and closing techniques.

So, there is a natural affinity for the *idea* of consultative selling. But what does that mean an agent is supposed to *do*? If you're wondering how to *do* consultative selling and how it's different from other kinds of selling, you're not alone. This chapter explores the meaning of consultative selling, and offers a unique methodology to help you learn to sell consultatively. That method is called Openhanded Selling.

Origins of Consultative Selling

The term "consultative selling" was originally coined by Mack Hanan in his 1970 book *Consultative Selling*. Throughout the 70's and 80's, Linda Richardson is credited with spreading the gospel of consultative selling as it pertains to discovering the pain a prospect is experiencing and advising them of a profitable solution.

The term consultative selling has been co-opted by many salespeople over the years. We now have real estate consultants, MLM consultants, insurance consultants, financial advisors, and many other sales professions with the term "consultant" or its cousin "advisor" in the title. Entrepreneurs who don't like to feel or sound like a carnival ticket hawker grab hold of the term "consultative selling" and apply their own meanings to the concept:

- To some people, selling consultatively means educating prospects or offering free help with the *hope* that they will buy. This is barely even selling, since the salesperson doesn't close.

- To others it means *persuading* prospects that the salesperson's product or service is the solution they've been looking for.

Both of these interpretations miss a key point about consultative selling...that *consulting* means using your expertise to diagnose your prospect's needs, design a solution that works for them, then guide them in making a decision that's right *for them*. Your consultation is intended to determine not only if they have a need, but what sort of solution would serve them *best*.

> *"Openhanded Selling means creating the conditions for your prospects to make decisions that meet their needs. If your product or service is the obvious solution, a sale is made."*

How Consultative Selling Helps You Sell Better

A Realtor called me to get help in preparing for a high-end listing appointment—to use me as a sounding board as she practiced her listing presentation. She spoke for a while, polishing her words until they glistened. When she was finished I said "That was great. But can you tell me why you decided your prospect needed *that* information?"

Realtor: "What do you mean?" she said. "That's my listing presentation. Everyone the seller meets with will have a listing presentation. If mine is the best, he'll hire me."

Me: "Yes," I agreed. "But how do you know that particular information in you presentation will make him want to hire you?"

Realtor: "Well, I don't know for sure, so I try to cover all the bases so that he can see that I offer a full range of services. It's designed to be convincing. Wasn't it?"

Me: "How do you know that your presentation will be more convincing than your competitors?"

Realtor: "Uh, well, I don't. I just have to do my best, right? Is there something else I can do?"

Me: "Well," I said. "Let me ask you some questions. Has your client ever sold a house before?"

Realtor: "Yes."

Me: "Do you know what he liked and didn't like about that experience?"

Realtor: "Well, no."

Me: "Do you know if he's excited about moving or worried?"

Realtor: "I'm not sure. His wife just died. Maybe he's sad."

Me: "Do you know if anyone else—any family or friends—are giving him advice?"

Realtor: "No."

Me: "Do you think if you knew that information it would help you consult with him more effectively? Maybe then you can tailor your presentation to better fit his exact situation."

Many salespeople are so tied up in making a persuasive presentation that they fail to ask the questions that make their presentation relevant.

> *"Openhanded Selling isn't JUST about finding and filling needs. It's about helping people make decisions that work for them. The only way to do that is to diagnose the deeper issues behind the decisions."*

How Consulting Works (in a Nutshell)

Since we're talking about *consultative* selling, what can we learn from the field of consulting that helps us improve our sales results? The central tenets of consulting are diagnosis, design, and recommendation.

Diagnosis: A consultant analyzes his client's situation to diagnose what's behind his problems. He doesn't simply *ask* his client what's wrong, because the issues are often hidden and complex. The consultant is an expert about knowing *where to look* for root causes and how to ask the *right kinds of questions* to surface them.

Design: The consultant is also an expert at working with his clients to develop solutions the client can integrate successfully into his idiosyncratic environment. In other words, the consultant knows that one solution does not fit all. He poses and explores ideas with his client to better understand the client's constraints. He helps his client see from different perspectives and adopt new strategies.

Recommendation: Finally the consultant is ready to make final recommendations. By this time, he's pretty sure what the client will accept or not, and how to position the recommendations to ensure they are implemented. He doesn't walk up to a client and say, "You need this," and expect the client to roll over. He makes his recommendations so that they are in exact alignment with what the client has already accepted during the consultation.

How is this like a sales consultant? Well, a good sales consultant will diagnose, too. Like a consultant, he'll recognize that a person's need is not just *driven* by something, it's also *held in place* by something.

For example, do you have any needs that you aren't solving? Any weight issues? Any organizational, family, or financial issues? What do you think is holding those needs in place—keeping you from solving them—despite the fact that you know you *need* to do something?

A good sales consultant will not just identify needs, he'll identify what's stopping his prospects from solving their need and he'll help them sort out the issues and come to a place where they can make a decision to move forward.

If the issues are complex or deeply rooted, the consultant will have to be talented in his use of questions and information to move prospects toward a decision. If the issues are simple, prospects will make decisions quickly. For example, when converting a lead to an appointment, the decision is a simple one that only requires a few questions. You can easily prepare for appointment-getting conversations like this in advance:

Prospecting in the Furniture Store

Lori is in a furniture store looking at new couches. She's testing a big leather sectional while a couple is testing some reclining chairs in the same suite of furniture. They strike up a conversation about furniture. Since Lori always wears her name tag in public, they can see she's a Realtor.

They ask about the market. Lori's antenna goes up and she kicks into consultant mode...not Realtor mode.

Lori: *"Market's good or not so good, depending on which side of the fence you're on. Are you buying or selling?"* (Lori is ready to respond to this common question.)

Couple: *"Well, we're looking at property up in Oregon and thinking about when it would be a good time to sell our house here. So I guess both."* (They discuss Oregon for a few minutes, finding common ground. Lori uses this conversation to discover whether or not they're well connected in Bend, where they want to move. She's uncovering needs.)

Lori: *"I know some smart agents in Bend, where you're moving. Do you have someone there looking out for your interests?"* (Lori is both telling and asking, using an influence technique where you state the benefit, then ask them if they want it.)

Couple: *"No. Can you give us their names?"*

Lori: *"My pleasure. There are a lot of moving parts when doing a double move like this, so every bit of help is important. Now, on this end, would it be worthwhile to set an appointment with me to talk about timing the sale of your home here, so you're ready when you find something in Oregon?"* (At first, Lori is expanding on the benefit of what she's offered. By pointing out that there are a lot of moving parts, she's emphasizing the complexity as a way of positioning her next question. Next, Lori gives information in the form of a question. The question keeps her in control of the conversation. If she had started pontificating about marketing timing and preparing a house for market, she would have run the risk of losing their interest.)

Couple: *"We'd like that."*

Hidden Background Issues Create Objections

The reason people raise objections is that *either* they don't see the value in what we're offering *or* they have a lot of background issues holding the issue in place. Or both.

If we're lucky, our prospect sees the value in what we're offering (how it satisfies their need) and there are no issues holding their need in place. Then the sale is easy. But that is seldom the case.

Furniture Example continued...

Suppose the couple had said, *"Well, we're not ready to make any decisions yet."*

Lori would know that something is holding their concern in place. To find out what it is, or to move past it, Lori can do one of two things:

She can assume she understands the underlying concern and power through with conviction. For instance, Lori could say, *"These kinds of decisions take a lot of time, especially when you've lived in a house for a decade or more and raised a family there, and put your love and life into it. Even so, the farther in advance you start to gather information, the more you'll make on the sale of your home, and in the end, it's about the investment you made and how it will help you in the next phase of life."*

Or she can ask more questions. *"What has prevented you from making decisions about this so far?"* *"What criteria would you use to determine when you'll be ready?"* If you find yourself in a situation where you don't have a ready and convincing story as in option one above, you may have to rely on these kinds of questions, which you can memorize in advance.

Even when a person sees tremendous value, there are often issues that prevent them from buying. These "objections" or concerns are sometimes known to the prospect, but often even the prospect doesn't know why they don't want to do something yet.

Home Buyer Example

Joseph is out looking at Open Houses with his Realtor. He has his loan lined up. He's ready to buy.

Joseph's real estate agent finds him the perfect house. She educates him about the market, location, and value. She creates scarcity by telling him he's going to lose the house if he doesn't act quickly.

But Joseph drags his feet. He's not sure. He can't decide.

So his agent educates him more about the housing market. She shows him how quickly houses are selling in that neighborhood. She gives him all the information he needs to understand why he must act quickly or lose the house.

Still he drags his feet. She asks him why he won't make a decision. He says he's just thinking about it and wants to be sure. So the agent gives him still more information to help him be sure.

What the agent doesn't know is that Joseph's girlfriend is pushing him to buy, while his mother is telling him to slow down. He's feeling pushed around by the women in his life. Joseph isn't really conscious of this, but it's making it difficult for him to be decisive.

He's not interested in more information about the housing market. That won't help him make a decision.

What will help Joseph make a decision? He needs someone to help him process his thoughts so he can get clarity before he'll move forward.

By asking the right kinds of questions, the agent can draw Joseph out and help him "process" his thoughts, supporting him in making a decision. The alternative is for the agent to lose him by allowing him to fade away or grow frustrated.

You can significantly reduce or eliminate objections by helping your prospect process background issues before you present your product. This isn't easy at first, mainly because it's not particularly intuitive.

Consultative Selling Is Not Intuitive

Good selling is non-intuitive. Bad selling is intuitive. Let me explain.

When faced with someone's need, most of us respond intuitively by providing a solution. Someone says, "I can't get the gum off my shoe." We say, "Have you tried alcohol?" Cause and effect. Quid pro quo.

This is such an ingrained part of our nature that some people will try to provide solutions even when they don't have any. (Maybe you have some mildly annoying friends who have to be "right" all the time or have an answer for everything.)

This is also true in selling, where we respond intuitively to needs by leaping to present our product or service solutions at the first opportunity. For example:

- A prospect says, *"My carpet is always dirty."* So the carpet cleaner says, *"Oh, well, did you know my carpet cleaning service will..."*

- A prospect says, *"I'm not sure now is a good time to buy a house."* So the real estate agent says, *"Well, let me tell you why I think it's a good time to buy..."*

- A prospect says, *"I hate my job. I'm thinking of going into business for myself."* So the Network Marketer says, *"You know, for just a few hundred dollars, you could get started in..."*

If the prospect isn't interested, or raises objections, the salesperson pitches harder, figuring he's just not being persuasive enough.

Alternatively, the non-intuitive thing to do when faced with a sales opportunity would be to back off. Instead of leaping on the opportunity, it would be to ask valuable questions and offer help with no strings attached.

For instance, suppose a carpet cleaning prospect says, *"My carpet is always dirty."*

The carpet cleaner responds, *"Oh, I can recommend some great Do It Yourself remedies. What sort of stains do you generally get?"*

This approach makes dead sales managers roll over in their graves...and gives live ones heartburn. They say things like, "Are you crazy? Why would you teach a sales rep to pass up an opportunity to sell?" As masters of the persuasive argument, they see only one way to sell, and that is to leap on an opportunity.

Yet when you think about it, offering something and asking questions makes perfect sense. By offering something of value, you're leading with the giving hand. That gives you the chance to open up the conversation and build credibility. Instead of feeling pushed, the prospect feels pulled, or invited. He'll start talking about his stains. The carpet cleaner will learn thing. Perhaps the owner was just talking about one little spot and doesn't really want a carpet cleaning. Maybe he will realize after talking to the carpet cleaner for a while that his stain problem is bigger than he thought, and he'll ask for help.

If you find yourself feeling pushy or *salsey* when you sell, it's likely that your intuition is telling you one thing, and your feelings are telling you another. Your intuition is saying *"I just heard an opportunity. I should sell now!"* Your feelings are saying, *"Yikes, I don't want to feel pushy. I don't like selling."*

To bring your feelings into alignment with your intuition, you'll have to gain the skill of creating a conversation that sells. This Openhanded Selling approach may feel non-intuitive at first, but that will quickly change as you see how easy it is and how relaxed you feel…and when you start making more money.

Hands Off…the Hourglass Metaphor

Another way to look at the process of Openhanded Selling is to imagine an hourglass.

Imagine turning over the hourglass at the beginning of a sales conversation. The sand falls through a narrow aperture into the bottom of the hourglass at a slow a steady pace. You can't rush it, just as you can't rush a sale.

Consider the top of the hourglass to be your customer's thought-processing time where you help her clarify the issues and address background noise that might be holding her needs in place. Consider the bottom of the hourglass to be your presentation time.

While the sand is in the top of the hourglass, focus on helping the customer clarify her needs and sort through her issues...be detached from the outcome, and don't push her into "admitting" she needs your product.

She may already know she needs it...that won't help her make a decision to buy it. By helping her address the issues out loud, chances are you'll be able to move her to a decision to buy sooner rather than later. At the very least, you will understand the true nature of any hesitation and be able to either work on those issues or walk away without spending great amounts of time with the *hope* she'll eventually buy.

When the sand has dropped to the bottom of the hourglass (after you've reached a point where she's expressing curiosity or interest in what you have to offer), it's time to present.

The Openhanded Selling Methodology

Openhanded Selling is both a mindset and a set of skills. The mindset is that of a consultant, or even a counselor...detached from the outcome, helping someone get past their issues so they can see the value of your solution.

And like a strong consultant or counselor, you will be able to influence this conversation dramatically by learning these six skill sets:

1. Transitioning from interest to appointment using a particular irresistible question sequence.

2. Using question chains to move the conversation deeper and forward at the same time.

3. Using a Socratic approach to raise and address objections proactively.

4. Crafting clean questions to remove the subtle innuendo, implication, and manipulation that pushes prospects away.

5. Presenting with units of conviction that build layers of value.

6. Closing with permission.

The master Openhanded Salesperson is skilled at converting leads and fulfilling complex relationship sales, is self-confident and relaxed, and enjoys a steady, peaceful flow of business.

Conclusion

Openhanded Selling is an alternative approach designed to meet the needs of non-traditional salespeople...people who don't see themselves as sales professionals, but still want the wealth and lifestyle that comes with being able to motivate others to buy.

The actual methodology requires more training than provided in this introductory chapter. If you are interested in learning Openhanded Selling, please contact Linda Schneider by email at: **contact@agentsonfire.com**.